The Rosetta Stone, whose three scripts clearly
corresponded to three versions of a single text, was to
provide the key to deciphering ancient Egyptian
hieroglyphics.

PTOLMYS

PTOLEMAIOS

P T O L M Y S

KL E O P A T R A

Excitement mounted among the Oriental-language
specialists. The Greek text, which reproduced a decree of
King Ptolemy V, appeared to be a translation of the
other two. The pharaoh's name must appear therefore in
the hieroglyphic version, surrounded by a cartouche.
From the Greek Ptolemaios, Jean-François Champollion
(1790-1832) identified the eight symbols that
constituted the hieroglyphic form. In 1822, on the
Philae obelisk, he found Ptolemy's cartouche again,
along with Cleopatra's. By comparing them, he
established the phonetic value of four signs, and was
then able to attribute an alphabetical value to the others.

By counting the number of hieroglyphs (1419) and words in the Greek text that corresponded to it (486), Champollion realized that this was not a purely ideographic script, with each sign representing a word, but a script that was

both ideographic and phonetic, in which only certain signs – those indicated here by a dot – were intended to be read. A typical sentence (above) reads: 'He says: the one who has come in peace, and has traversed the heavens, is Ra.'

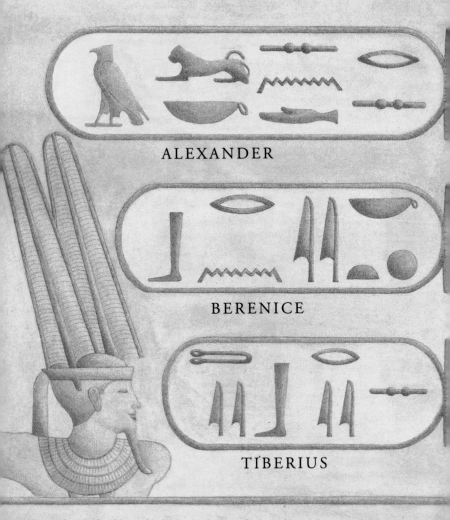

ALEXANDER

BERENICE

TÍBERIUS

Using the twelve hieroglyphs he had identified in the Ptolemy and Cleopatra cartouches, Champollion began deciphering all the cartouches, from the Rosetta Stone and other monuments, of which he had copies. Working on twenty-four names, he successively deciphered those of Alexander, Berenice, Tiberius, Nero, Vespasian and Trajan.

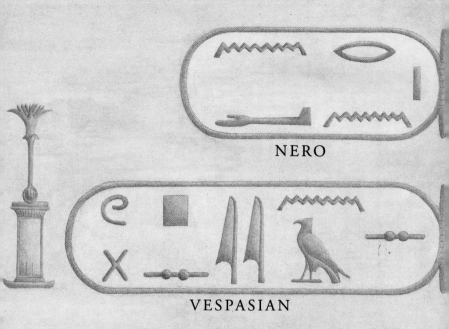

NERO

VESPASIAN

TRAJAN

Champollion had established the correct method. On 27 September 1822 he sent the Académie des Inscriptions et Belles-Lettres a letter announcing his discovery, the *Letter to Dacier, concerning the Alphabet of phonetic Hieroglyphs used by the Egyptians to engrave the Names of the Greek and Roman Sovereigns on the Monuments.* This document marks the birth of Egyptology.

TUTHMOSIS

Champollion's one concern now was to continue deciphering more and more names. He had to be absolutely certain that the alphabet thus established held good for all the pharaonic texts. On other copies of texts sent from Egypt he was able to make out the names of Tuthmosis and Ramesses: the hieroglyphic riddle had been solved. A few years later he was to achieve his dream of sailing to Egypt and reading on the spot all those texts which had fascinated

RAMESSES

Europeans for centuries. At Deir el-Bahari, a painted relief showed a pharaoh offering a sacrifice; above his raised arm the cartouche enclosing his name identified him as Tuthmosis III, *c.* 1450 BC. At Thebes a painting in the tomb of a young prince represented a king in state costume. This, according to the cartouche, was King Ramesses III, father of Prince Amenhirkhopshef, who was buried there in *c.* 1150.

CONTENTS

THE SEARCH FOR ANCIENT EGYPT

Jean Vercoutter

THAMES AND HUDSON

By the 4th century Christianity was the major religion in the Byzantine Empire, and in AD 391 the Emperor Theodosius I decreed the closure of all pagan temples throughout the Empire. In Egypt probably no more than a handful of people still worshipped the ancient gods and goddesses, but the closure of the temples had a further, unexpected, consequence: the hieroglyphic script, until now a living tradition, suddenly ceased to be understood.

CHAPTER 1

THE DISAPPEARANCE
OF PHARAONIC
EGYPT

Marble bust of Alexander, who conquered Egypt in 332 BC and founded Alexandria. After his death (323 BC), Ptolemy I had his body brought back to Egypt.

The priests not only presided over daily worship, they also gave instruction in the language and the scripts which were indispensable for the observance of religious rites. When those priests disappeared there was no one left who could read the texts carved on the monuments or written on papyrus and preserved in the libraries.

Flames engulfed the library at Alexandria, and with it the history of ancient Egypt

Theodosius' decision was all the more serious in its effect because of a much earlier event: when Julius Caesar captured Alexandria in 47 BC the library had been burnt. Approximately 700,000 works, including many relating to pharaonic Egypt, are said to have been destroyed – among them, the thirty-volume *History of Egypt* which Ptolemy I commissioned the priest Manetho to write in Greek.

In 48 BC the conflict between Pompey and Caesar reached its climax. Defeated at Pharsalus, Pompey fled to Egypt, but was murdered when he landed at Alexandria on the orders of Ptolemy XII, who had quarrelled with his sister Cleopatra and was hoping to make an ally of Caesar. This did not deter Caesar from occupying the royal palace, where he summoned the two protagonists to a parley.

Manetho's work, drawn from authentic Egyptian texts held in libraries and temple archives, retraced events from earliest antiquity and described the customs and religion of his country's inhabitants.

Before the invention of printing, copies of books had to be made by hand. Any big library possessed the unique copy of many works, and in the case of Alexandria, these were kept in the library attached to the temple of Serapis, in Alexandria itself. Unfortunately, in AD 391, this temple was not merely closed, but burnt down, with the result that those works that had escaped the disaster of 47 BC now disappeared in their turn.

By *c.* AD 450, not only did no one read or understand ancient Egyptian texts any more, but everything that the Egyptians themselves had written in Greek, as a means of introducing their country to its foreign occupiers, had been lost.

Gold, silver and bronze coinage was introduced by Ptolemy I.

Fearing assassination by one of Ptolemy's soldiers stationed in Alexandria, Cleopatra arrived at the palace by boat, concealed inside a carpet. Caesar was amused and took her part against her brother. Alexandria rose up in revolt. Fearing that the rebellion would spread to the fleet, Caesar had all its ships set alight. The fire reached the city, and the library, a legendary centre of learning, was accidentally completely destroyed. Much later its memory was to be recaptured by romantic painters like Luigi Mayer, whose imaginary view of the library ruins (1804) is seen here.

This wall painting from Herculaneum (1st century AD) depicts a ceremony in honour of the goddess Isis. A priest, dressed in a white linen tunic, steps out of the temple, flanked by two acolytes each shaking a sistrum (rattle), used to accompany ritual singing and dancing. Isis, sister and wife of Osiris, god of the dead, was the most popular goddess in ancient Egypt, revered for her magical powers and worshipped in a great many temples, the most famous being that at Philae. Thanks to the Greeks and the Romans, the cult of Isis spread beyond the Nile valley, not only to Italy, but also to Gaul and Britain, where there was a temple to her in Roman Londinium.

Despite the closure of the temples and the two fires in Alexandria, not everything relating to the Egypt of the pharaohs was lost

Classical writers, both Greek and Latin, took an interest in Egypt, and their works have been preserved in Rome and in Byzantium. Moreover, the history of the Israelites from the 2nd millennium BC was often linked to that of Egypt, with the result that several books of the Old Testament, such as Genesis and Exodus, retain fragments of Egypt's political history as well as alluding to the customs of its people. Again, as a means of proving the authenticity of the Old Testament, source of the Christian religion, the Church Fathers, who were familiar with Manetho's work, frequently cited passages from it in their own. It is from Manetho that modern Egyptologists have adopted the division of Egyptian history into thirty dynasties.

Fascinated by its very strangeness, the Greeks and Romans based many of their traditions on the religion of the pharaohs. The cult of Isis, for example, was celebrated throughout the Roman Empire (particularly

The Exodus from Egypt and Crossing of the Red Sea (opposite centre). After witnessing the plagues that had befallen his country, Pharaoh granted Moses and the Israelites permission to go and celebrate the Passover in the desert. He soon changed his mind, however, and sent his army in pursuit of them. The waters of the Red Sea opened to allow the Israelites to cross, but when the Egyptian army tried to follow, the waters closed again and engulfed them.   Exodus 14

in Gaul), as were those of Osiris and Anubis.

It is thanks to Plutarch's detailed *De Iside et Osiride* (*On Isis and Osiris, c.* AD 100) that we know the details of the Osiris legend, since the original Egyptian texts generally did no more than allude to it.

Via the Bible in particular, many legendary episodes relating to ancient Egypt have thus been handed down to us. The stories of the Red Sea crossing; of Joseph sold by his brothers into slavery; of Joseph at Pharaoh's court; of the infant Moses abandoned in a basket on the Nile and

Obelisk of Tuthmosis III outside St John Lateran, Rome (below). Obelisks were solar symbols placed on either side of a temple entrance.

adopted by Pharaoh's daughter – all helped to keep the memory of ancient Egypt alive during the Middle Ages and the Renaissance.

Numerous monuments were plundered by Roman and Byzantine emperors in order to beautify their own cities, and their strange inscriptions exerted a powerful effect on people's imaginations. The obelisks brought to Rome and erected in various of the city's squares, such as the Piazza del Popolo and the Piazza della Minerva, inspired the Jesuit priest Athanasius Kircher (1602-80) to try and unlock the secret of the hieroglyphic script at the beginning of the 17th century.

But it was above all the accounts of travellers which, feeding a curiosity already inflamed by the mysteries of Egypt, were to have a decisive influence on the birth of Egyptology.

The first visitors to Egypt came from the coasts of Palestine and Syria. Their visits are recorded in a number of Egyptian wall paintings, though the foreigners themselves left no account of their impressions. It is to those inquisitive and tireless travellers, the ancient Greeks, that we owe the first descriptions of the Nile valley.

CHAPTER 2

TRAVELLERS IN ANCIENT TIMES

Each god was thought to inhabit the earth in the form of a sacred animal: Horus as a falcon, Hathor as a cow, Bastet as a cat. The animal was kept in the temple itself and, when it died, it was mummified (like this cat) and buried in a special cemetery.

In the *Odyssey* Homer describes a raid by Greek pirates – one of whom was Odysseus – in the Nile Delta. After killing the men and rounding up the women and children to sell as slaves, the Greeks suddenly found themselves surrounded by a band of Egyptians, and were either massacred or taken prisoner in their turn.

Pirates were followed by mercenaries and traders. In their clashes with the Assyrians, and later the Persians, the pharaohs of the 26th dynasty recruited most of their mercenaries from the Greek colonies, in particular Ionia. Greek traders came to settle in Egypt, at Naucratis in the Nile Delta, or near military garrisons, at Elephantine for example, where they enjoyed the pharaoh's protection.

For all their excellence as soldiers, the Greeks were unable to prevent the defeat of the Egyptian army at Pelusium (525 BC) at the hands of the Persian king Cambyses. In becoming Persian, Egypt did not close its doors to foreigners; quite the opposite, for the Persians were masters not only of Egypt, but of the whole of Asia Minor, and their subjects included the Greeks of the Ionian coast and neighbouring islands.

Herodotus, one of the greatest of all travellers, arrived in Egypt in *c.* 450 BC

Prior to leaving his home at Halicarnassus in Asia Minor, Herodotus had taken the trouble to read everything the Greeks had ever written about Egypt, and he was all the better prepared for a fruitful visit since he had, and openly expressed, a sympathy for the Egyptians themselves. His account of Egypt forms Book 2, an important part of his *History.* Very often details that appeared to derive from an overly vivid imagination or from misinformed sources have proved to be true, and Herodotus continues to be used, with care, as a reference

Wall painting (*c.* 1900 BC) in the tomb of Prince Khnumhotep, 'Overseer of the Eastern Tribes', at Beni Hasan. It depicts a group of Bedouins, led by their chief, Absha, arriving in Egypt. Fifteen foreigners in all are shown, the youngest children mounted on a donkey, but the text indicates that there were thirty-seven in total.

work by Egyptologists today.

All the same, the most useful pieces of information are not those relating to political history, but the remarks on daily life, religion, and the country itself, observation and description being Herodotus' forte. Thanks to him, we

Wall painting (*c.* 1420 BC) from the tomb of Sobekhotep at Thebes. It shows Syrian chieftains dressed in long robes offering the king gifts of gold and silver vases inlaid with semi-precious stones. One of the chieftains is holding his young daughter by the hand.

know about the life of the ancient Egyptians in the sort of detail which it is beyond the scope of the pictorial material and the inscriptions to convey or explain. Everything Herodotus encountered in this foreign country became for him a matter for wonder. Thus he notes: 'Everywhere else, priests of the gods wear their hair long; in Egypt they are shaven. With all other men, in mourning for the dead those most nearly concerned have their heads shaven; Egyptians are shaven at other

times, but after a death they let their hair and beard grow.' One brief statement – and the riddle of the pharaoh with a stubbly chin is solved. Painted on a fragment of white limestone, this fine portrait is clearly a study of the new pharaoh in mourning for his predecessor; but without Herodotus no one would have guessed.

Herodotus may make rather arbitrary connections between Egyptian and Greek gods, but he also gives us valuable information on the popular religious festivals he himself attended. Here, for example, is his description of the annual festival at Paprêmis in the Nile Delta: 'At Paprêmis sacrifice is offered and rites performed as elsewhere; but when the sun is sinking, while a few of the priests are left to busy themselves with the image, the greater number of them beset the entrance of the temple,

This unshaven chin of a pharaoh suggests that he was in mourning for his predecessor.

with clubs of wood in their hands; they are confronted by more than a thousand men, all performing vows and all carrying wooden clubs like the rest. The image of the god, in a little wooden gilt casket, is carried on the day before this from the temple to another sacred chamber. The few who are left with the image draw a four-wheeled cart carrying it in its casket; the other priests stand in the temple porch and prevent its entrance; the votaries take the part of the god, and smite the priests, who resist. There is hard fighting with clubs, and heads are broken, and as I think (though the Egyptians told me no life was lost), many die of their wounds.'

Herodotus was especially interested in the animal cults so popular in Egypt at the time of his visit. 'Some of the Egyptians hold crocodiles sacred,' he writes, 'others do not do so, but treat them as enemies. The dwellers about Thebes and the lake Moeris deem them to be very

Nile crocodile at Thebes, watercolour by Sir John Gardner Wilkinson. Crocodiles, abundant in ancient Egypt, no longer live along the Egyptian stretch of the Nile. By the time of Napoleon's expedition in 1798, travellers had to go as far as Thebes to see one.

sacred. There, in every place one crocodile is kept, trained to be tame; they put ornaments of glass and gold on its ears and bracelets on its forefeet, provide for it special food and offerings, and give the creatures the best of treatment while they live; after death the crocodiles are embalmed and buried in sacred coffins. But about Elephantine they are not held sacred, and are even eaten.'

Thanks to Herodotus' vivid descriptions, the ancient Egyptians come alive for us, while paintings and reliefs in the temples and tombs frequently confirm the accuracy of his observations.

Egypt became a Hellenized country, and the people themselves the sole guardians of the manners, customs and religion of earlier times

Roman artists were fond of depicting imaginary Nile landscapes, like this mosaic representing the Upper Nile.

The very different accounts by Greek and Roman writers who came after Herodotus are valuable in their own way, for Egypt was still ancient Egypt and, as the conscientious tourists that they were, these chroniclers read whatever reference material was available (and is now lost) before leaving.

Diodorus Siculus, a contemporary of Julius Caesar, was typical of the new, well-informed traveller, but in his account of his Egyptian travels it is difficult to distinguish the things he had read from the things he himself saw or learnt in conversation with Egyptians. More credulous than Herodotus, he accepted unquestioningly the Egyptians' claim that rats were born from Nile mud. Though he rarely comments on a direct experience, he notes that the peasants at harvest time cut the first ears of corn, thresh them and make an offering of them to the goddess Isis. Like all newcomers to Egypt, Diodorus was astonished by the animal cults and comments that in time of famine the Egyptians have eaten one another rather than touch a sacred animal.

Mummy fragment. Numerous mummies were stolen, broken up and crushed into powder which was sold as a universal remedy until the end of the 18th century.

Strabo, a Roman citizen whose mother was Greek (the language in which he wrote), was born by the Black Sea. He visited Egypt *c.* 30 BC, fifty years or so after Diodorus, when Egypt was a province of the Roman Empire. Thanks to his friendship with the governor, Aelius Gallus, Strabo was able to travel about the country with the greatest ease, and he devoted an entire book of his *Geographica* to his trip. Like Herodotus, he jots down impressions and anecdotes, describing with amusement the religious festivals he has witnessed: 'Some writers go on to record the cures, and others the virtues of the oracles there. But to balance all this is the crowd of revellers who go down from Alexandria by the

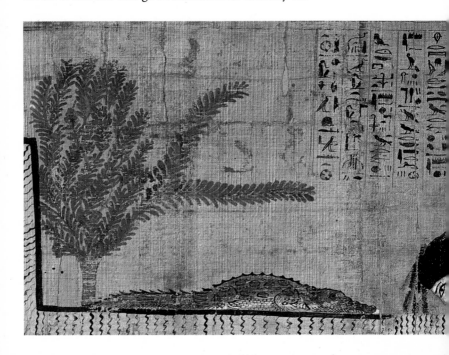

O ther objects were sometimes used to simulate the dead animal, as in the case of this crocodile (left): only its head is real, the body being made of bound palm branches. The body of a dog (below) is formed into a cylindrical shape with a separate upper section sewn on to represent the head.

canal to the public festivals; for every day and every night is crowded with people on the boats who play the flute and dance without restraint and with extreme licentiousness, both men and women, and also with the people of Canobus itself, who have resorts situated close to the canal and adapted to relaxation and merry-making of this kind.'

Like his predecessors, Strabo was fascinated by the animal cults

He gives very precise details. During a visit to Crocodilopolis, in the Fayuum, he notes for example: 'for the people in this Nome hold in very great honour

T he Chantress of Amun, Here-ubekhet, prostrates herself before a crocodile, embodying the earth god Geb and not, as is usually the case, the god Sobek.

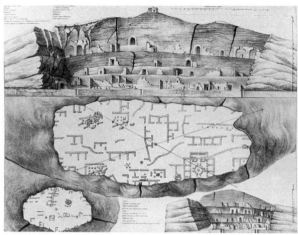

Cross-section and plan of the town of Crocodilopolis as seen by J.-J. Rifaud when he cleared the site in 1823. Shortly after his arrival in Egypt, in 1812, he devised a systematic plan of campaign that led to the discovery of 6 temples, 66 statues and more than 200 inscriptions.

the crocodile, and there is a sacred one there which is kept and fed by itself in a lake, and is tame to the priests. It is called Suchus; and it is fed on grain and pieces of meat and on wine, which are always being fed to it by the foreigners who go to see it. At any rate, our host, one of the officials, who was introducing us into the mysteries there, went with us to the lake, carrying from the dinner a kind of cake and some roasted meat and a pitcher of wine mixed with honey. We found the animal lying on the edge of the lake; and when the priests went up to it, some of them opened its mouth and another put in the cake, and again the meat, and then poured down the honey mixture. The animal then leaped into the lake and rushed across to the far side; but when another foreigner arrived, likewise carrying an offering of first-fruits, the priests took it, went around the lake in a run, took hold of the animal, and in the same manner fed it what had been brought.'

Strabo's information is so precise that on the basis of it Auguste Mariette was to discover the temple and tombs of the Apis Bulls, the Serapeum, at Saqqara.

Another famous traveller was Plutarch (1st century AD), priest of the Delphic Apollo

When Plutarch went to Egypt, Alexandria still had copies of Manetho's writings. It was from the three works Manetho had devoted to the religion of the

One of two massive seated statues of Amenophis III (the 'Colossi of Memnon') that stood before his mortuary temple at Thebes. The northern one was said to moan at dawn and dusk. The Greeks claimed that it was their own hero Memnon speaking through the statue, saluting his mother Eos, goddess of the dawn. Restorations *c.* AD 200 put an end to the sound.

pharaohs that Plutarch took the primary material for his own extensive work on Isis and Osiris. Rather than conveying his own impressions in the manner of Herodotus and Strabo, he merely verified the facts as Manetho had related them. Nevertheless, it is to Plutarch that we owe our detailed knowledge of the cult of Osiris, most famous of the Egyptian gods.

Of the Roman emperors, two, Hadrian and Septimius Severus, had their names carved on the northern statue of the Colossi of Memnon in memory of their visit. Other emperors only demonstrated their interest in Egypt by having temples to its gods built or restored in their own name, without ever actually visiting the country. Only Germanicus went to Egypt in 19 BC in order to see its ancient monuments for himself. He visited the temples of Thebes in the company of an old priest who was able to translate the hieroglyphic texts into Latin and Greek (which Germanicus, like all educated Romans, could speak). Thanks to this priest, and to Tacitus, who noted his remarks, we have some idea about 'the tribute-list of the subject lands ... the weight of gold and silver, the numbers of weapons and horses, the temple-offerings of ivory and spices, the quantities of corn and other materials contributed by every country'.

In AD 125, Hadrian's young favourite, Antinoüs, drowned in the Nile and the emperor founded the town of Antinopolis in his memory. Some impressive ruins, including the column erected by Severus Alexander, were still standing in 1789, but in 1828 Champollion found only rubble there.

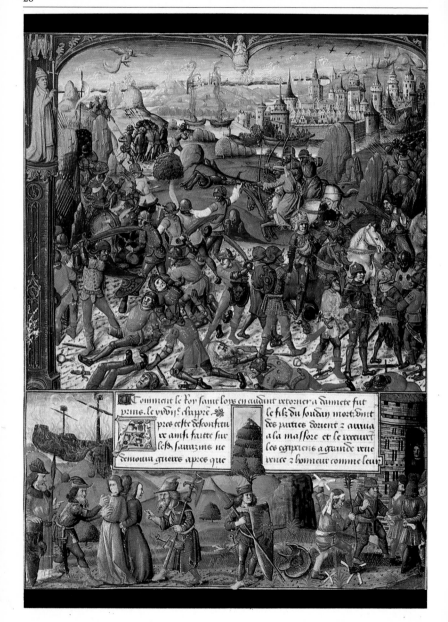

Comment le roy saint loys en audant retorner a damiete fut
pris, le xxviij.e chappitre. pres ceste desconfitu
re ainsi faitte sur
leSz sarrazins ne
demoura gueres apres que

le filz du souldan mort, dont
des parties dorent z arriua
a la massore et le recoeurt
les egiptiens a grande reue
rence z honneur comme leur

None of the accounts from the 1st to the 14th centuries can compare with those of the ancients. At the time of the Crusades, we find fresh accounts of Egypt and its monuments from travellers, but now no one could read the hieroglyphic texts. Since Egypt was a Muslim country, moreover, it was difficult to gain access to it, and the Europeans who actually succeeded scarcely ever got beyond Cairo.

CHAPTER 3

CRUSADERS, MONKS AND SIGHTSEERS ON THE BANKS OF THE NILE

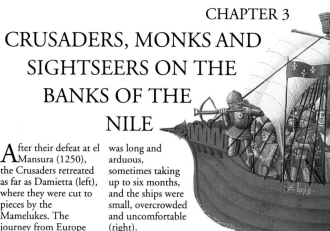

After their defeat at el Mansura (1250), the Crusaders retreated as far as Damietta (left), where they were cut to pieces by the Mamelukes. The journey from Europe was long and arduous, sometimes taking up to six months, and the ships were small, overcrowded and uncomfortable (right).

Consequently, travellers during the late Middle Ages and the Renaissance mention only the Nile Delta and its towns, primarily Damietta and Rosetta, or the pyramids of Giza – which they, nourished on the Bible, identified as 'Joseph's granaries'. What interested them were those traces that remained here of an earlier Christian presence, rather than the Egypt of the pharaohs. Besides which, very few of them stayed longer than a fortnight: more often than not, Egypt was merely a staging post on the pilgrim route to or from the Holy Places.

It was not until the 17th century that the really serious expeditions began; and not until Napoleon's expedition in 1798 that Egypt could finally be said to have been 'rediscovered'.

Monks travelled to the Near East to preach the Christian Gospel

From the early 17th century, Capuchins, Dominicans and Jesuits had established more or less permanent centres in the Near East, and in Cairo in particular, from which they could branch out to preach the Gospel.

In 1672 Father Vansleb, a Dominican priest of German origin, arrived in Cairo. Louis XIV's chief minister, Jean Baptiste Colbert, had entrusted him with the task of buying manuscripts and ancient coins, and he now travelled up and down the country, even venturing as far as Upper Egypt.

The pyramids, as depicted in (top) Sébastien Munster, *Cosmography*, and (bottom) A. Kircher, *Œdipus Aegyptiacus*. In the 17th century visiting the pyramids was an entire expedition in itself. Father Vansleb wrote: 'On 27 April [1672], the French consul and I went there together. We had three janissaries to protect us. There were accordingly about fifty of us mounted on donkeys, equipped with four days' supplies.'

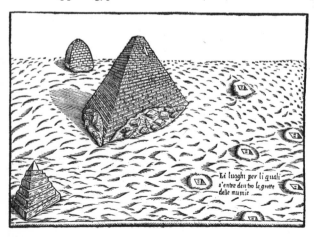

Li luoghi per li quali s'entra dentro le grotte delle mumie

Like his fellow Catholic missionaries, Vansleb was attracted by the old Coptic monasteries, and he visited the White and Red monasteries at Sohag, as well as the monastery of Saint Anthony, on the Red Sea. But he also took an interest in the ancient monuments, being the first European to describe the ruins of Antinopolis, the Roman town built by Hadrian in memory of his young favourite, Antinoüs, who drowned in the Nile. On his return to France, Vansleb found himself in disgrace; Colbert refused to reimburse his expenses, and he died a few years later, disillusioned and penniless.

Jean de Thevenot (1633-67) was the first 17th-century traveller drawn to the ancient Near East by sheer curiosity

Thevenot went as far as India and, in 1652, he stopped off in Egypt. Like his Renaissance predecessors, he saw only the Nile Delta, Cairo and its environs. He took the measurements of the Great Pyramid at Giza and described its interior. He was also the first to suspect that the ancient capital of Memphis must be located in the vicinity of Saqqara, where he discovered a stone sarcophagus 'entirely covered in idols and hieroglyphs'.

The Coptic monastery of Saint Simeon at Aswan is one of the largest in Egypt; monks' cells, refectory and church are enclosed within an outer wall. The monastery was probably abandoned in the 14th century.

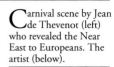

Carnival scene by Jean de Thevenot (left) who revealed the Near East to Europeans. The artist (below).

Like his contemporary Vansleb, Thevenot was particularly interested in Egyptian mummies. Vansleb had a pit opened up at Saqqara and found a room at the bottom, full of jars containing mummified birds. He took half a dozen away with him. In another pit he found two coffins, but recounts his disappointment on seeing their contents: 'We found nothing of any note and we left them where we had found them.' Thevenot depicts the same operation in this illustration (left) from his *Account of a Journey in the Levant* published in 1664.

Benoît de Maillet, French consul-general in Egypt under Louis XIV, sent the king numerous antiquities

By virtue of his position, Maillet was the precursor of those infamous 19th-century consuls who looted Egypt's ancient monuments for the benefit of the large European museums.

As well as the king, Maillet supplied the Comte de Pontchartrain and in particular the Comte de Caylus, who himself had excavated sites in Greece. Most of the Egyptian antiquities in the Caylus Collection are now in the Bibliothèque Nationale's Cabinet des Médailles, Paris.

Maillet's memoirs formed the basis of a book published in 1735 and exhaustively entitled *Description of Egypt, containing many strange Observations on the ancient and modern Geography of this Country, on its ancient Monuments, its Morals, Customs, the Religion of its Inhabitants, on its Animals, Trees, Plants....* For the first time ever, Egypt was described in its entirety, with antiquities given pride of place. Maillet's cross-section of the Great Pyramid is fairly accurate, although disproportionately tall. Pre-empting General Antoine Desaix and Jean-François Champollion's idea of sending one of the Luxor obelisks to Paris, Maillet planned to transport back to the capital a truly worthy monument – Pompey's Pillar in Alexandria! – but had to give up the idea for practical reasons.

Drawing of Pompey's Pillar at Alexandria by Benoît de Maillet (left).

In 1735 Maillet published the first cross-section of the pyramid of Cheops at Giza (the Great Pyramid), accurate in all but proportions. While giving a description of the interior, he warns: 'With respect to the interior of the pyramid, it is so dim, and the walls are so blackened by the smoke from candles burnt there by visitors over the centuries, that it is difficult to judge the quality of the stones. . . . What one does notice is that they are highly polished, extraordinarily hard and so perfectly joined that it would be impossible to slide a knife point in the space that lies between them.'

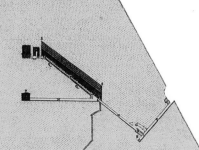

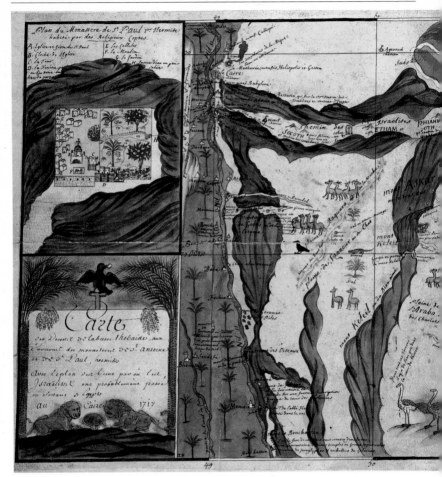

Father Claude Sicard (1677-1726), in charge of the Jesuit mission to Cairo, travelled throughout Egypt and made the first map of the country

Sicard was entrusted by the regent, Philippe d'Orléans, with the job of examining and drawing Egypt's ancient monuments, and was assigned a draughtsman for the purpose. He had taught humanities at the Jesuit college in Lyons and was an excellent Greek and Latin scholar,

All the illustrative material for Sicard's project – flora and fauna, sites of ancient monuments and plans of Coptic monasteries – was gathered during the desert crossing between Cairo and the Red Sea.

as well as being fluent in written and spoken Arabic. The emphasis of his work gradually shifted from a quest for ancient monuments to a study of the geography of ancient Egypt. As Champollion was to do a century later, Sicard used Greek, Latin, Coptic and Arabic texts to establish the former names of the towns and villages he systematically visited. Like all his fellow Jesuits, he knew how to handle a sextant and, with the help of this instrument, he drew up the first scientific map of Egypt

Watercolour map of Egypt by Sicard, 1717. He endeavoured to retrace the route of the Exodus on his journey.

from the Mediterranean to Aswan. The map, which has recently come to light again, was sent to the king in 1722 and showed the precise location of not only Memphis and Thebes, but also all the great temples, including Elephantine, Edfu, Kom Ombo, Esna and Dendera. When Sicard died of plague in Cairo in 1726, aged fifty, he had just completed his *Geographical Comparison of ancient and modern Egypt*.

The detailed information provided by Maillet and Sicard greatly facilitated future expeditions to Egypt, which no longer seemed like 'a vague and mysterious region peopled with savages, demons, magical snakes, pygmies and monsters'. Mention should also be made of two other influential travellers: Savary and Volney.

The upper entrance (above) of the pyramid at Chephren is cut into the northern face, at *c.* 15 m above ground level. From here a passage meets the corridor leading to the burial chamber.

At the end of the 18th century Egypt attracted more and more visitors

Savary travelled purely for his own pleasure. He was in Cairo from 1776 to 1779 and, whatever he himself says on the subject, never explored further afield. His *Letters Written from Egypt* refer more extensively to modern Egypt than to the ancient monuments, which he describes in terms taken from classical authors or from Maillet or Sicard. His account has its own charm, however, as shown by the following description of a visit to a pyramid (the Great Pyramid at Giza).

'At 3:30 in the morning, we arrived at the foot of the

largest. We left our coats at the entrance to the passage leading into the interior, and began the descent, each holding a torch. Near the bottom, we had to wriggle on our bellies like snakes in order to gain access to the inner passageway (the mirror image of the first). We shuffled up this [the Grand Gallery] on our knees, while pressing our hands against the sides. Failure to do this would have entailed the risk of slipping on the incline, and the slight grooves in its surface would have been insufficient to prevent us from sliding all the way down to the bottom. About halfway up, we fired a pistol shot and the deafening noise went on and on, echoing in all the recesses of the immense edifice. It disturbed thousands of bats, which hurtled up and down, striking us on our hands and face and extinguishing several of our torches.'

Savary accompanies his description with the cross-section of the pyramid, shamelessly lifted from Maillet. He goes on to describe the burial chamber and its sarcophagus, which had lost its lid and was still surrounded by 'fragments of earthenware vessels'. Savary's charmingly written *Letters* enchanted many members of the 1798 expedition who would later reproach him for having deluded them with descriptions of an Egypt that was no more than a fantasy land.

Chephren's lower entrance (above) is carved directly into the rock at ground level. A long subterranean passage leads from here to the burial chamber.

"We had scarcely gone a quarter of a league when we saw the summit of the two great pyramids. The appearance of these ancient monuments that have survived the destruction of nations, the fall of empires, the ravages of time, inspires a kind of reverence. The soul glances over the centuries that have flowed past their unshakeable bulk and experiences an involuntary shudder of awe. Let us salute these remains of the Seven Wonders of the World! And pay tribute to the might of those who raised them!" Savary

The catacombs at Alexandria (left). The Grand Gallery in the Great Pyramid, Giza (below and opposite).

Optimism, on the other hand, is not a characteristic of Volney's *Journey in Syria and Egypt*. Following a sound training in classics at Angers, Volney moved to Paris, where he studied medicine, and published in 1777, at the tender age of twenty, his *Report on Herodotus' Chronology*. He got to know the encyclopaedists Diderot, d'Alembert and Turgot and, in 1781, on inheriting some money, he decided to travel. 'I was attracted by the newly emerging America and by the American Indians, but for other reasons resolved on Asia. It struck me that Syria, in particular, and Egypt offered scope for the sort of political and social observation I was interested in making.'

So he left to make his observations, though not without first preparing himself (since he was not especially robust) by a programme of running, fasting, jumping over ditches and climbing high walls – to the astonishment of the inhabitants of Angers. When he decided that he was sufficiently fit, he left, with his pack on his back, his gun on his shoulder and a leather belt containing 6000 gold francs round his waist. This was no doubt the gear with which he disembarked at Alexandria in 1782, though from the moment of his arrival, our extraordinary traveller never once mentioned it again. His *Journey in Syria and Egypt* contains not a single description of Egypt, though he spent seven months there. It is worth quoting from, nevertheless, since it was widely read by the scholars on the 1798 expedition, who were struck by Volney's remarks regarding the ancient monuments: 'If Egypt had been in the hands of a nation kindly disposed towards the Fine Arts, it would yield material to further our knowledge of Antiquity such as the rest of the world can no longer offer. In point of fact, there are no interesting ruins left in the Nile Delta, because the inhabitants have destroyed everything, out of either necessity or superstition. But in the less populated Saïd [Upper Egypt] and at the less frequented edges of the desert, a few monuments remain intact. They are buried in the sands, stored ready for future generations to uncover. It is to such future generations that we must entrust our hopes and our desires.' Volney's vision was to be fulfilled much sooner than he had anticipated. His *Journey*, published in 1787, was the sole book Napoleon took with him to Egypt. Following its publication, Volney appears to have lost interest in Egypt. His life now took a series of dramatic turns. Elected representative of the Third Estate in 1789, he later became secretary of the Constituent Assembly. He was imprisoned during the Terror and risked execution. In 1795 he finally left for America, but was deported back to France in 1798 on charges of spying. Later Napoleon proposed making him a member of the Consulate, then Minister of the Interior, but Volney stood by his revolutionary ideals and refused both positions. Under the Empire he accepted a seat on the Senate. He died in Paris in 1820.

In 1798 Napoleon's soldiers – visitors of a very different kind – disembarked at Alexandria. And with them came Baron Dominique Vivant Denon

Baron Dominique Vivant Denon (1747-1825) was an extraordinary character. Born near Chalon-sur-Saône, he was a Gentleman of the Chamber under Louis XV, then First Secretary at St Petersburg and at Naples under Louis XVI. Though a member of the nobility, he survived the Terror. During the Directoire Josephine de Beauharnais took him under her wing. Thanks to her Denon joined the Egypt expedition, despite Napoleon's doubts about his age (he was fifty).

The pyramids of Giza

Of the Seven Wonders of the Ancient World, the Great Pyramid of Cheops (seen here on the left in a plate from Mayer's *Views in Egypt*, 1804) is the only one still standing today. It measures 230 m along the base of each side and covers an area of 5 hectares. Originally 146 m high, it is constructed of granite blocks 1 cu. m in 201 courses, the lowest, at the base, measuring 1.5 m in height, the succeeding courses graduating down to 55 cm at the summit. It is estimated that there are a total of 2.6 million blocks, weighing 7 million tons, in it. These were cut from neighbouring quarries, transported to the site and hoisted into place. Napoleon calculated that, by using material from all three pyramids, it would have been possible to encircle France with a defensive wall 3 m high and 30 cm thick! Little wonder that such extraordinary proportions should have given rise to a whole range of speculation.

The Great Sphinx. Man or lion?

To pilgrims and travellers, the Great Sphinx at Giza was every bit as mysterious as the pyramids. In 1735 Maillet described it as 'a woman's head grafted on to a lion's body' and wondered if it might perhaps represent 'an association of Virgo and Leo'. All the old drawings simply show the sphinx's vast head emerging from the sand. The task of clearing away the sand from its body began in 1816, under G. B. Caviglia's direction, was abandoned and resumed by Mariette in 1853. It was only in 1886 that Maspero and Brugsch fully extricated the body of the sprawling lion, guardian of the tomb of King Chephren. This and the next picture are also from Mayer.

From the heights of these pyramids...

The Great Pyramid was originally topped by a 'pyramidion' made of a single granite or basalt block, and on the blocks that served as a platform for the pyramidion, travellers and tourists were in the habit of carving their names. Despite the dangers, many visitors attempted the climb to the top. In 1581 Jean Palerme wrote: 'One gentleman eager to make the ascent did in fact reach the summit, but was astounded (overcome with giddiness), fell and was smashed to pieces. The crushed remains no longer looked like a human being.'

The Grand Gallery and the King's Chamber

Within the mass of limestone built up in horizontal layers, the builders of the Great Pyramid left a series of inner passages leading to King Cheops' burial chamber. An entrance in the north face, concealed by a large slab of granite, opened on to a narrow passageway that led to the lower end of the Grand Gallery. The gallery itself is huge (8.5 m high and 47 m long). It gives on to a level area, which leads into the King's Chamber. In the sarcophagus here, the mummy of King Cheops once lay, surrounded by precious objects. Despite all the builders' attempts to seal off the corridors and defeat the robbers, it was broken into on several occasions and everything was stolen. When travellers and local peasants subsequently ventured into the passages, they would climb the Grand Gallery by torchlight and gaze into the sarcophagus – now empty – of a king who died about 2600 BC.

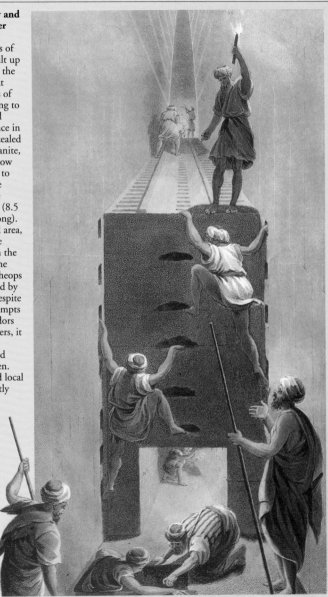

On his return from Egypt, Napoleon appointed him Director General of Museums, and it was Denon who founded the Musée Napoléon, now the Louvre. When the Empire fell, Louis XVIII recalled having seen Denon at Louis XVI's court and kept him on in his post. He remained in it until after 1815, when he voluntarily retired as a protest against the restitution (demanded by the allies) of works seized under the Empire. During his retirement, he wrote *History of Art from ancient Times to the Beginning of the 19th Century.* He died aged seventy-eight at Quai Voltaire in Paris, only a few yards from the Institut d'Egypte, of which he had been a member since 1787.

The birth of Egyptology owes a great deal to Vivant Denon, whose work *Travels in Upper and Lower Egypt* brought ancient Egypt to life once more. Published in Paris in 1802, it was immensely popular; it ran to forty successive editions and was translated into English in 1803 and into German. Denon's success was well deserved, resulting in part from his excellent draughtsmanship. He had followed the expeditionary force under Desaix despatched against the Mameluke Murad Bey in Upper Egypt, and it was then that he discovered Egypt's ancient monuments.

V ivant Denon was just beginning his career under Louis XV when he painted this self-portrait in typical late 18th-century style.

The aesthete forced to submit to the hardships of a military campaign

Nothing, however, dampened Denon's enthusiasm and

he carried on drawing, even when the conditions were extraordinarily difficult, as he himself explains: 'Here the pitiless reader, sitting quietly in his study with his map before him, will say to the poor, hungry, harassed traveller, exposed to all the trouble of war: "I see no account of Aphroditopolis, Crocodilopolis, Ptolemais – what is become of all these towns? What had you to do

A fantasy portrait of Vivant Denon in the rôle of scholar-sage, surrounded by antiquities from the Louvre collections.

there, if you could not give any account of them? Had you not a horse to carry you, an army to protect you?" But, kind reader, please to recollect, that we were surrounded with Arabs and Mamelukes, and that, in all probability, I should be made prisoner, robbed, and very likely killed, if I had thought proper to venture only a hundred paces from the column to fetch some of the bricks of Aphroditopolis.'

An anecdote, picked out by Anatole France, sums up the sort of conditions in which Denon had to work: 'One day while the flotilla was travelling upriver, he saw some ruins and said he must do a drawing of them. Obliging his companions to set him down, he hurried out into the plain, ensconced himself in the sand and began drawing. Just as he was finishing, a bullet whizzed past his piece of paper, and he looked up to see an Arab who, having missed his target the first time, was in the process of reloading. He snatched up his own gun, shot the Arab through the heart, shut his portfolio and went back to the boat. In the evening, when he showed his drawing to the general staff, General Desaix said: "Your horizon isn't straight." To which Denon replied: "Ah, that's the fault of that Arab. He fired too soon."'

It was sketches executed in conditions such as these that served as the basis for Denon's engravings in *Travels in Upper and Lower Egypt*. While undoubtedly less

"In 1797, at a ball given by M. de Talleyrand, he met a young general. The general asked for a glass of lemonade and Denon passed him the one he had in his hand. The general thanked him and they started a conversation... within a quarter of an hour he had struck up a friendship with Napoleon Bonaparte. Mme Bonaparte took an immediate liking to him and he became one of her close circle of friends. The following year he was asked: 'Would you like to join the Egyptian expedition?' 'Will I be able to dispose of my own time and be free to come and go as I choose?' he asked. He was assured that he would. 'Then I'll go', he said. He was over fifty at the time.**"**

Anatole France

precise, they are much more evocative than those contained in the later *Description of Egypt*, and they were to give European readers a clear idea of the number, richness and beauty of the monuments scattered across Egypt. Scholars, like Champollion, and looters in search of a fortune succumbed to the so-called Egyptomania they unleashed.

Headquarters established by Desaix (above) in the tombs near Nagada. Denon is sitting on the far left; in the centre, General Belliard is preparing to arbitrate between a group of Arabs from Nagada and some persons accused of stealing.

Denon (below) sketching the ruins of Hierakonpolis.

On his return to Cairo in July 1799, Vivant Denon gave Napoleon an account of everything he had seen, and showed him his illustrations. The future emperor then set up two special commissions of scholars whose task it was to measure and draw all the monuments observed by Denon, and to continue his researches. These commissions gathered the raw material for the massive *Description of Egypt.*

CHAPTER 4
TREASURE
HUNTERS AND
THIEVES

Napoleon exhorted his men before the Battle of the Pyramids, Giza (July 1798): 'Soldiers, from the heights of these pyramids forty centuries are watching you '; he appears on horseback at the far right.

Published in Paris between 1809 and 1822, the nine volumes of text and eleven large volumes of illustrations of the *Description* completed and elaborated Vivant Denon's pioneering work and provided the foundation for all future studies in Egyptology.

Europe rediscovered Egypt

It is hard to imagine today the feverish excitement

The Commission des Sciences et des Arts de l'Armée d'Orient. Their clothes – heavy green frock coat, close-fitting breeches and felt hat – were totally unsuited to the Egyptian summer.

prompted by the dual publication of Denon's work and that of the Commission des Sciences et des Arts de l'Armée d'Orient, as the scholars who wrote the *Description of Egypt* were collectively known. Egypt became fashionable literally overnight. Between 1802 and 1830 a dozen travellers of note came from France, England, Germany and Switzerland to see for themselves the wonders revealed by the *Journey* and the *Description,* and the accounts and drawings they brought back from their travels in two years helped to maintain the momentum of Egypt's growing popularity.

This obsession had one unexpected consequence: the looting of antiquities. The government of Mohammed Ali (1769-1849), viceroy of Egypt, tolerated such activities, or was even directly responsible for them. On the positive side, such thefts supplied the documents from different eras which were to help the scholars uncover the secret of the hieroglyphic script.

Between 1798 and 1801 numerous objects, like these bronze figurines, were taken to the Institut d'Egypte in Cairo. Many of them were later seized by the British.

The temple of Qasr-Qarun (left) at the north-west end of the Fayuum. 'View at sunset. To the right, the French engineers' caravan, headed by their Arab guides and accompanied by an escort. To the left, the camp of a hostile tribe hidden behind the dunes.' The temple (1st century BC) was part of the town of Dionysias, which also boasted a Roman fortress.

The façade of Qasr-Qarun (centre). 'The intention is to show the monument in moonlight. The travellers are on the point of entering the building in the company of their guides. The caravan is camped on the right.' The plan of the temple (above) was drawn by a M. Bertre, 'engineer and geographer, former captain'. (Similar commentaries accompany all the illustrations in the *Description of Egypt*.)

Such pillaging was nothing new. The treasures housed in the tombs had tempted others before

As early as 2000 BC King Merikare confessed to his son: 'There has been fighting in the burial grounds, and the tombs have been looted. I have done such a thing myself.' In 1100 BC the mayor of Thebes discovered that the royal tombs were being systematically looted by organized gangs, who were sharing the booty between them. The matter was judged in Thebes, and the many records (on papyrus) that have come down to us reveal the subsequent course of events.

The commission of inquiry appointed by the mayor began by examining all the royal tombs: 'Pyramid tomb of Sebekemsaf [1700 BC], son of Ra. It was apparent that this had been broken into by the robbers, who had dug a tunnel to gain access to one of the chambers of the pyramid from the outer hall of the tomb of Nebamun, inspector of granaries to King Menkheperre [Tuthmosis

III]. The body had been removed from the royal burial chamber. The same was true for that of his wife, Queen Nubkhaes.'

The commission concluded by charging numerous workmen or petty officials with theft, almost all of them being associated with the administration of the necropolis. Arrested and summoned to appear before the court, they swore an oath to tell the truth, on pain of 'having their nose and ears cut off, or being put to death'. One of them declared: 'Four years ago, in the 17th year of the king, my master, we broke into the tomb of King Sebekemsaf and searched it. We opened the outer coffins, then the inner ones. We found the noble mummy of the king dressed as a warrior; it had numerous amulets and gold ornaments round its neck, and its gold headdress was in place. The noble mummy was covered with gold from head to foot, and the inner

Silsila. 'View of the caves dug at the entrance to the old quarries. A large boat has anchored in front of the caves. Beyond them lie the sandstone quarries. Columns and sculptures are carved out of the rock. In the middle ground is a single rock surmounted by a large crown. A chain is said to have been attached to this rock, barring ships from sailing any further down the Nile, but there is no substance to the claim.'

Description of Egypt

Champollion spent some time at Silsila in 1829, correctly establishing the date of the large central chapel as 18th dynasty (*c.* 1350 BC). The purpose of the chain, if it did indeed exist, would have been to prevent Nubian ships from entering Egypt. Stone from the nearby quarries was used to build the temples at Karnak and Luxor.

Lower half of a limestone ushabti (below), from *Description of Egypt*.

coffin was inlaid with a great deal of gold and silver, both inside and out, and with all sorts of precious stones. We took the gold from on top of the mummy, as well as the amulets and ornaments from round its neck. We [also] stole all the goods that we could find – gold, silver and bronze objects, that is – and we shared out everything between us, in eight lots.' The inquiry concluded: 'The

Small temple on the island of Elephantine, drawn by Denon (left). When Champollion stopped at Elephantine, less than thirty years later, the temple had gone, its stones probably used to produce lime.

evidence and the court rulings were duly recorded and sent to the king.' (He alone had the authority to pass a death sentence.) Trials of this kind take up yards and yards of papyrus, and even then not all the written material has come down to us! They demonstrate how widespread such robbery was, and give an idea of the lavish contents of the royal tombs, as the discovery of Tutankhamun's tomb in 1922 confirmed.

The looting continued. There were even manuals offering tips on how to do it

The pillaging that had begun with the Egyptians themselves continued under the Roman and Byzantine emperors, who removed numerous monuments, obelisks, sphinxes and statues for the purpose of decorating their capitals, Rome and Constantinople, or simply their private villas. Hadrian and Diocletian were both culprits in this respect. And even before them, Persian kings had robbed the temples of their statues.

Looting was not confined to the consuls' agents. This watercolour by Sir John Gardner Wilkinson shows a peasant woman searching for antiquities in a Theban tomb.

In transforming the temples into churches and taking over the rock-cut tombs, the Copts and hermits were simply guilty of a different kind of pillage: the destruction, mutilation or effacing of paintings and reliefs. The belief that temples and tombs were places where treasure and rich burial goods were secreted seems to have formed part of an oral tradition in Egypt, transmitted from generation to generation.

A manual written in Arabic, of which several known copies exist, the *Book of Buried Pearls and of the precious Mystery, giving Indications regarding the Hiding Places of*

Finds and Treasures, provides a detailed list of the whereabouts of the hidden treasure, along with the magic formulas necessary for outwitting its formidable guardians, the *jinn*. Treasure hunters were so numerous in Egypt that in the 14th century the activity came to be regarded as a craft! Copies of the *Book of Buried Pearls* were still changing hands at the beginning of the 20th century, and in 1900 an Egyptian conservator at the Cairo Museum declared: 'This work has been responsible for destroying more ancient monuments than either war or the onslaught of the centuries'.

Trading in antiquities began in Cairo in the early 19th century, with local peasants acting as the suppliers. In this illustration by Luigi Mayer a wealthy Egyptian is being shown a sarcophagus complete with mummy and a statue.

In the 19th century no laws existed against looting

When, after 1810, collectors and explorers began
stripping Egypt of its ancient monuments, they were
merely following a long-established tradition, and their
activities were greatly facilitated by the government of
Mohammed Ali. Born in Macedonia (then a Turkish
province) in 1769, Mohammed Ali joined an Albanian
corps, becoming its commander in 1803, when the
English left Egypt. In 1805 the Turkish sultan appointed
him governor of Egypt, and in 1811 he had all those
Mamelukes who contested his authority massacred in the
citadel at Cairo – an event which has been widely
recorded in the history books.

From now on, and though still in principle answerable
to the sultan at Constantinople, to whom he owed his
appointment, Mohammed Ali was in practice sole ruler
of Egypt. Resolving on a programme of modernization
for his country, he hired numerous self-styled
'technicians' from England, France, Germany and
elsewhere, in order to create the industry Egypt lacked. It
was from the ranks of such hardened adventurers that
those recruits would be drawn who, from 1810 to 1850,
were responsible for despoiling Egypt of a great number
of its ancient monuments.

Foreign consuls in Egypt played a pivotal role in the
up-and-coming trade in antiquities. The reason for this
was simple. Excavation and transportation required
local manpower, and manpower, like the land itself,
belonged to the viceroy, Mohammed Ali. His
authorization thus had to be sought if workmen were
to be recruited. It came in the form of a written
document known as a *firman* (a Persian word
meaning 'order'). The consuls were
better placed than anyone to
obtain a *firman:* they could
request an audience with the
viceroy whenever they chose,
and he often needed their
help too, if only in shipping
over from Europe the
machines on which his
country's growing industry
depended.

Mameluke horsemen,
watercolour by Sir
John Gardner
Wilkinson. An élite
mounted corps in the
Turkish army, they lost
their powerful status
under Mohammed Ali
(1769-1849).

Mohammed Ali was
appointed Turkish
viceroy of Egypt in 1805.
His modernization plans
led to the construction of
factories and shops but
many ancient
monuments were
destroyed.

Consuls-general like Sweden and Norway's Giovanni Anastasi, France's Bernadino Drovetti, Jean-François Mimaut and Raymond Sabatier, and England's Henry Salt first had to acquire their *firmans*, then recruited agents among the foreign adventurers who came to seek their fortune in Egypt. These agents excavated or bought antiquities in the consuls' name, and took charge of their removal from the site.

The Drovetti Collections can be seen today in Paris, Turin and Berlin

Bernadino Drovetti (1776-1852), a naturalized Frenchman originally from Piedmont in north-west Italy, had served as a colonel during the 1798 expedition, and in the course of some rather fierce fighting, had saved the life of Napoleon's future brother-in-law, Joachim Murat. He returned to Egypt as vice-consul in 1803, and was appointed consul-general in 1810. In that post he came into contact with Mohammed Ali. When

Engraving of Drovetti and his team (*c.* 1818) from Forbin, *Journey in the Levant.* The ex-consul is holding a plumb line in front of the face of a colossus. The European dressed in oriental costume and leaning against the statue is Jean-Jacques Rifaud. The figure on the right of the picture is wearing his hair in typical Nubian style.

Drovetti (below) had served as a colonel in the French army in Egypt and never lost his martial air.

Drovetti's and Salt's collections form the core of the Egyptian sections in the Turin, Paris, London and Berlin museums. This splendid black granite statue of Tuthmosis III (1490-1436 BC) in the Turin Museum bears an inscription stating that the sculptor Rifaud had found it at Thebes in 1818 while in Drovetti's employ. It was part of Drovetti's first collection, which Louis XVIII turned down.

Louis XVIII acceded to the throne in 1814 and Drovetti lost his position he was able to stay on in Egypt and, thanks to the viceroy's protection, pursue his lucrative career as a trader in antiquities. The Bourbons were prepared to overlook his Bonapartism, and in 1820 Drovetti was reinstated as consul-general, remaining in that position until 1829.

Drovetti took an active part in the search for antiquities and personally directed the excavation work, but it was his unscrupulous agents (guaranteed impunity by the *firman*) who were responsible for the most shameless looting. The most adept was Jean-Jacques Rifaud, a sculptor from Marseilles who was to spend forty years in Egypt, and had the habit of engraving his name – in splendid lettering, at that – on the Egyptian statues he procured for Drovetti. Whenever a quarrel broke out between Drovetti's and Salt's men, 'quick as lightning and red as a turkey cock, Rifaud hurled himself between the sparring groups, unleashing a torrent of abuse and, finally, when they persistently failed to understand his Provençal, lashing out at them with his stick'.

As the years went by, the antiquities piled up in the courtyard at the consulate. When he decided he had enough, Drovetti proposed to Louis XVIII that he buy

An inscribed sarcophagus and boats on the Nile; two of some 4000 drawings produced by Rifaud in his forty years in Egypt.

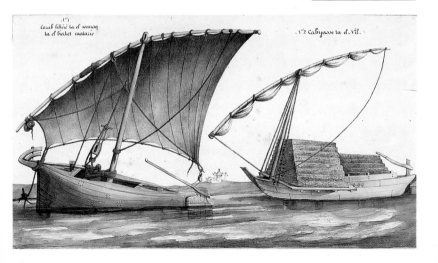

them for the Louvre, but the king refused, reckoning the price too high, and this first Drovetti Collection was finally bought, in 1824, for 400,000 lire, by the king of Sardinia. The Turin Museum (to which it went) thus became the first in Europe to own a really good collection of Egyptiana. It included, among other magnificent pieces, the intact statues of Amenophis I, Tuthmosis I, Tuthmosis III and Amenophis II, a sphinx of Amenophis III and, most notable of all, the seated figure of Ramesses II. This huge granite statue, which appears in all the histories of Egyptian art, carries on its base the inscription: 'Discovered by J. Rifaud in the service of M. Drovetti, in Thebes, 1818'. The collection includes more than a thousand artefacts and monuments, which Champollion was to use, in 1825, to check the accuracy of his method of deciphering hieroglyphs.

Satisfied with the results of his first commercial venture, Drovetti continued his excavations and brought together a second collection. He again offered it to France. On Champollion's recommendation, Charles X bought it, for 250,000 francs, for the Louvre, where it formed the core of the museum's Egyptian section. The collection includes a marvellously

Since there were no mechanical means available for lifting or hauling the monuments (many of them weighing several tons), hundreds of fellahs – Egyptian peasants – were employed to shift them as far as the Nile. They were then loaded on to boats and transported down to Alexandria, from where they were shipped to Europe.

worked solid gold cup given to one of his generals by Tuthmosis III.

Drovetti went on to assemble a third collection, which was bought in 1836 by the king of Prussia, on the recommendation of the Egyptologist Karl Richard Lepsius. Though smaller than the first two (it cost only 30,000 francs), it included some fine pieces.

As a reward for his exploits in Palestine (*c.* 1455 BC), Tuthmosis III presented General Djehuty with this gold cup, which is now in the Louvre. According to an Egyptian folk tale, Djehuty had captured the town of Joppa (modern Jaffa) by concealing his soldiers inside earthenware jars. The *Arabian Nights* tale 'Ali Baba and the Forty Thieves' was no doubt based on the same story.

Henry Salt was also responsible for the removal of thousands of Egyptian artefacts

While Drovetti was busy exploring Thebes and Tanis, the English painter Henry Salt was being equally energetic. From 1802 onwards, he had travelled extensively in the East, illustrating the books published by wealthy

View of Mount Barkal from Lepsius, *Discoveries in Egypt and Ethiopia.* In 1844, during a trip to the Sudan, Lepsius removed a monumental statue of a ram, representing Amun the protector of Amenophis II (*c.* 1450 BC), from the great temple of Amun, at Gebel Barkal. The methods he used were the same as Belzoni's, and ninety-two Nubian peasants were required to complete the job. The statue is now in the Berlin Museum.

fellow countrymen on their return home. From 1809 to 1811 he stayed in Abyssinia, a country to which it was particularly difficult to gain entry. Appointed consul in Egypt in 1816, he immediately began following Drovetti's example. Though more confined to Cairo than Drovetti, he was assisted by agents every bit as active as the French consul's. Among them was a Greek from Lemnos by the name of Athanasi, better known to travellers of the time as Yanni, and, most notably, the extraordinary Giovanni Battista Belzoni.

Salt assembled his first collection in 1818 and offered it to the British Museum. The museum bought it, but only after haggling over the price and agreeing to pay a paltry £2000, a sum which did not even cover the costs of excavation and transport. The Trustees of the museum rejected Salt's best piece, the alabaster sarcophagus of Seti I, and he subsequently sold it to a

Portrait of Henry Salt by J.J. Halls.

private collector, Sir John Soane, for the same price as the rest put together.

Salt assembled a second, much more important collection, which he again offered to the British Museum. Put off no doubt by the attitude of the Trustees, in 1824 he sold it instead to Charles X of France, for the sum of £10,000 (250,000 francs). The Salt Collection, together with the second Drovetti Collection, put the Louvre on a par with the Turin Museum. According to the museum's inventories, Salt's collection comprised 4014 pieces, notably a section of wall covered with inscriptions from Karnak, the pink granite sarcophagus box of Ramesses III (to the mortification of Drovetti, Belzoni had the lid and presented it to the Fitzwilliam Museum, Cambridge), two large granite sphinxes and a granite naos from the temple at Philae.

Salt, who was an artist by profession before becoming consul-general, painted this splendid view of Greater Cairo (below) from the citadel in the 1820s. The three mosques in the foreground were built by (from left to right) sultan Hassan (14th century), El Mahmudiya, and the Emir Akhor (16th century).

Like Drovetti, Salt brought together a third collection, but it was not sold until after his death (in Egypt) in 1827. Most of its 1083 items were purchased by the British Museum.

A cursory visit to the museums in London, Paris or Turin reveals that what the consuls and their agents were primarily looking for were the larger, more impressive monuments, which were usually made of granite: obelisks, sphinxes, sarcophagi and colossal statues. These enormously heavy objects had to be removed from their resting place – often a tomb carved deep into the rock – and then hauled on to the riverbank and hoisted on to simple feluccas without the mechanical assistance of pulleys or cranes. In Alexandria they then had to be transferred on to small sailing ships (steam ships did not exist prior to 1830).

Giovanni Belzoni, man of impossible missions

The undisputed master of these difficult operations was the Italian Belzoni, Salt's main agent. Like Vivant Denon, he was something of an eccentric. Born in Padua in 1778, Belzoni left for Rome at the age of sixteen, and at the time of the French invasion in 1798, he was thinking of becoming a monk. In 1803 he went to London, where he earned a living on the music-hall stage. He was tremendously strong and tall (over two metres apparently) and was billed as the 'Patagonian Samson', appearing in 'Patagonian' costume, with a tall feathered headdress. The highlight of his act was the 'human pyramid', in which Belzoni came on stage strapped into an iron harness with a dozen people perching on it.

Belzoni went from England to Portugal and then to Spain. In 1814 he was in Malta, where he met an agent of Mohammed Ali who suggested that he came to Egypt and put to use his knowledge of hydraulics (which he had studied as a young man). Accompanied by his wife and an Irish servant, Belzoni left for Egypt the same year and immediately met up with Drovetti

Belzoni (above) as the 'Patagonian Samson' at the Sadlers Wells Theatre, London, 1803, and (below) in Turkish dress in 1820.

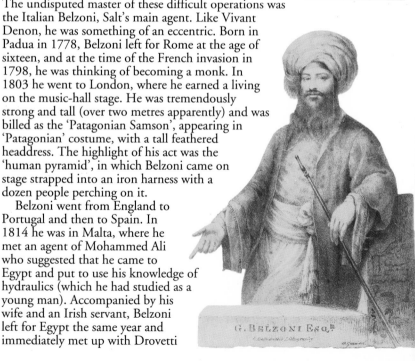

G. BELZONI Esq.ᴿ

and the Swiss explorer J.L. Burckhardt (1784-1817).

Belzoni spent the next two years perfecting a water wheel designed to facilitate irrigation. He showed it to Mohammed Ali, but vested interests at court prevented the viceroy from accepting his invention, despite the fact that it could supply six times as much water as the traditional saqiah wheel. It was a disaster for Belzoni, who had by now used up all his funds.

It was at around this time that Henry Salt was appointed consul-general of Great Britain in Egypt. Before he left London, Sir Joseph Banks, a wealthy collector and one of the Trustees of the British Museum, urged him to use his position to collect antiquities both for the museum and for Banks himself.

During a visit to Upper Egypt Burckhardt, meanwhile, had observed a colossal pharaoh's head lying in front of the temple in what the French scholars had named the Memnonium, that is, the Ramesseum. The local people confirmed that the French had made a vain attempt to remove the statue. Burckhardt suggested to Mohammed Ali that he might offer this monument to George IV, but the viceroy refused to believe that any prince would be grateful to him for a mere lump of stone! That was how matters stood when Burckhardt spoke about his find to Banks, and later to Belzoni.

From the Ramesseum at Karnak to the British Museum in London – a long journey for the bust of a king

Now that his water-wheel project – and with it his means of earning a living – had failed, Belzoni suddenly

In *Egypt and Nubia* Belzoni tells his life story: how, among other things, he presented his water wheel to Mohammed Ali, and how, with the help of a machine invented by Faraday, he gave Mohammed Ali an electric shock which threw him into the air.'The machine was set to work; and, although constructed with bad wood and bad iron, and erected by Arabian carpenters and bricklayers, it was a question whether it did not draw six or seven times as much water as the common machines. The Bashaw, after long consideration, gave his decision; and declared, that it drew up only four times as much. It is to be observed, that the water produced by this machine was measured by comparison with the water procured by six of their own; and that, at the time of measuring, the Arabs urged their animals at such a rate, that they could not have continued their exertion above an hour; and for the moment they produced nearly double the quantity of water, that was usually obtained....The business ended in this manner; and all that was due to me from the Bashaw was consigned to oblivion, as well as the stipulation I had made with him.'

remembered the head in the Memnonium, and he and Burckhardt went to see Salt to discuss the idea of removing it. Mindful of Banks' remarks, Salt gave Belzoni the money for the removal of the head, plus a sum to purchase as many antiquities as he could find.

Belzoni left Cairo at the end of June 1816. Arriving in Thebes on 22 July, he hurried to the Ramesseum. 'As I entered these ruins, my first thought was to examine the colossal bust I had to take away. I found it near the remains of its body and chair, with its face upwards, and apparently smiling on me, at the thought of being taken to England. I must say, that my expectations were exceeded by its beauty, but not by its size.'

He began his preparations for removing the head. 'All the implements brought from Cairo to the Memnonium consisted of fourteen poles, eight of which were employed in making a sort of car to lay the bust on, four ropes of palm leaves, and four rollers, without tackle of any sort.'

On 24 July, armed with his *firman*, he went to the *Kashif* (regional governor) to request the assistance of

"This day we removed the bust out of the ruins of the Memnonium. To make room for it to pass, we had to break the bases of two columns."

Belzoni
Egypt and Nubia, 1820

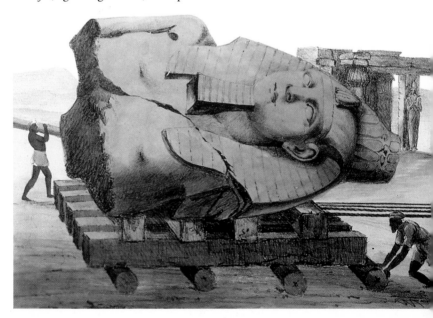

twenty-four workmen. The governor observed that no workmen were available and that it would be better to wait until after the floods.

Belzoni was insistent and eventually bribed the *Kashif* into promising him some men for the following day. But the next day dawned and no men arrived. There were more comings and goings, more promises and more gifts. Finally, on 27 July, a handful of men did in fact turn up, but not enough. However, when the others saw them working, it was not difficult to persuade them to follow their example. 'The carpenter had made the car, and the first operation was to endeavour to place the bust on it. The Fellahs of Gournou [Gourna], who were familiar with Caphany, as they named the colossus, were persuaded that it could never be moved from the spot where it lay; and when they saw it moved, they all set up a shout. Though it was the effect of their own efforts, it was the devil, they said, that did it; and, as they saw me taking notes, they concluded that it was done by means of a charm.... By means of four levers I raised the bust, so as to leave a vacancy under it, to introduce the car; and, after it was slowly lodged on this, I had the car raised in

Belzoni was also an excellent artist and his notes recording his day-to-day activities are supplemented with marvellous watercolours, like this one showing how the bust of the young Memnon was transported from the Ramesseum. They were later published as a series of lithographs.

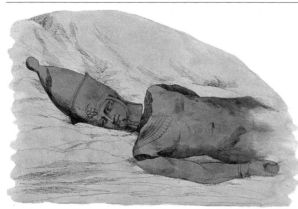

Colossus found at Karnak. 'On my return from Gournou, I had the pleasure to find the discovery had been made of a colossal head, larger than that I had sent to England. It was of red granite, of beautiful workmanship, and uncommonly well preserved, except one ear, and part of the chin, which had been knocked off along with the beard. It is detached from the shoulder at the lower part of the neck, and has the usual corn measure, or mitre, on its head. Though of larger proportion than the young Memnon, it is not so bulky or heavy, as it has no part of the shoulder attached to it. I had it removed to Luxor, which employed eight days, though the distance is little more than a mile.' Belzoni, *Egypt and Nubia*

the front, with the bust on it, so as to get one of the rollers underneath. I then had the same operation performed at the back, and the colossus was ready to be pulled up. I caused it to be well secured on the car, and the ropes so placed that the power might be divided. I stationed men with levers at each side of the car, to assist occasionally, if the colossus should be inclined to turn to either side....'

'Lastly, I placed men in the front, distributing them equally at the four ropes, while others were ready to change the rollers alternately. Thus I succeeded in getting it removed the distance of several yards from its

Ramesses II, 'the young Memnon' (opposite), retrieved by Belzoni, is in the British Museum.

Interior of the temple of Amun at Karnak. 'I seemed alone in the midst of all that is most sacred in the world; a forest of enormous columns, adorned all round with beautiful figures, and various ornaments, from the top to the bottom.' Belzoni, *Egypt and Nubia*

original place. According to my instructions, I sent an Arab to Cairo with the intelligence that the bust had begun its journey towards England.'

Thanks to Belzoni's account in his *Narrative of the Operations and Recent Discoveries within the Pyramids, Temples, Tombs and Excavations, in Egypt and Nubia* (1820), we can follow the party's halting progress towards the Nile. It took them ten days to cover little more than 1200 metres! But at last, on 5 August, they had almost reached their destination. Belzoni was overjoyed: 'Accordingly, I went to the place early in the morning, and, to my great surprise, found no one there except the guards and the carpenter, who informed me that the *Kaimakam* [deputy governor] had given orders to the Fellahs not to work for the Christian dogs any longer.' This was serious. The river could flood at any moment, and it would then be impossible to move the bust for several months. Belzoni went straight to the *Kaimakam* to demand an explanation.

The *Kaimakam* claimed that the order had come from the *Kashif* himself. So, Belzoni went to the *Kashif.* More discussions, another gift ('two splendid English pistols'),

In the 19th century, the ruins of Karnak were in such disorder that anyone could wander in and remove statues, reliefs or whatever caught his fancy. The ruins were the scene of outright battles between the Drovetti and Belzoni factions. One day, when he was riding a donkey across the site, Belzoni was set upon by Drovetti's men and would probably have been seriously hurt had it not been for Drovetti's intervention.

and written permission was granted for work to be resumed. On 7 August the workmen returned, and on the 12th, without further setbacks, the bust of Ramesses II finally reached the Nile. Now all Belzoni had to do was to send it by boat to Cairo. While waiting for a vessel large enough for the job, he took advantage of his enforced idleness to go and visit the Valley of the Kings. Then he went to Nubia and saw the two temples at Abu Simbel, promising himself that some day he would return and find a way inside. At Philae he acquired a small obelisk. Back in Luxor in November, there was no sign of the promised boat. After further negotiations and payment of the sum of 3000 piastres (about £70 at today's values), the boatmen agreed to supply it. While preparations were under way, Belzoni began excavations in Karnak, where he found eighteen lion-headed statues (representing the goddess Sekhmet), a kneeling statue of Seti II and a number of sphinxes, all of which he would ship back with the bust.

On 17 November the bust had been hoisted on board, to the amazement of the Gourna Arabs, who had expected to see boat and all subside beneath the waves.

Belzoni's drawing shows the state the Karnak ruins were in. In the foreground is the First Pylon; on the left the column of Taharqa with the Second Pylon beyond; on the right the temple of Ramesses III and the series of pylons that lead to the road to Luxor.

Belzoni at Abu Simbel

Burckhardt had discovered Abu Simbel in 1813. Fascinated by his descriptions of it, Belzoni resolved to go there himself and be the first to get inside. In September 1815 his boat drew level with the two temples: the Small Temple, on the right of his drawing, identifiable by the six colossal figures decorating its façade, and the Great Temple, situated halfway along the cliff. Belzoni noted his impressions on stepping closer: 'The sand from the north side, accumulated by the wind on the rock above the temple, and which had gradually descended towards its front, choked the entrance and buried two-thirds of it. On my approaching this temple, the hope I had formed of opening its entrance vanished at once; for the amazing accumulation of sand was such, that it appeared an impossibility ever to reach the door.'

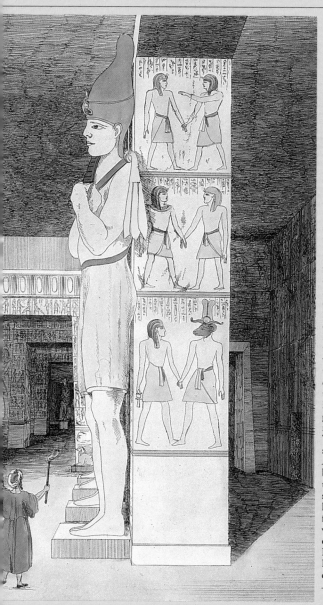

The Great Temple reveals its secrets

Belzoni returned the following year in the company of three Englishmen, Captains Irby and Mangles (both RN) and Henry Beechey. They were determined to clear the entrance to the temple. It took three weeks' work before the four men found the temple entrance and were able to slide down the sand into the interior: 'From what we could perceive at the first view, it was evidently a very large place; but our astonishment increased, when we found it to be one of the most magnificent of temples, enriched with beautiful intaglios, painting, colossal figures, etc.' Belzoni describes the three side chambers, which were decorated in the most brilliant colours, then notes that the heat was such (44 ° C in fact) that they had great trouble in even making a few sketches. The four men ran out of supplies and had to leave Abu Simbel on 3 August, but as souvenirs they took with them 'two life-size lions with hawks' heads, a small sitting figure, and some copper work belonging to the doors' (all now in the British Museum). Belzoni had hoped for even greater wonders.

In the tomb of Seti I

Even tombs were transported back to Europe. But copies were also made. After discovering the tomb of Seti I and its magnificent alabaster sarcophagus in the Valley of the Kings, Belzoni had the idea of producing exact copies of the tomb paintings. When they were exhibited in London, at the Egyptian Hall in Piccadilly, these life-size colour reproductions attracted such enormous crowds that the 'Paduan Titan', as Belzoni was called in France, decided to exhibit them in Paris too. By a curious coincidence, the barge carrying the paintings across Paris passed by the Institute building on 27 September 1822, at the very time that Champollion was there reading his letter to the Académie announcing that he had unravelled the secrets of the hieroglyphic script. The exhibition of the tomb of Seti I in the Boulevard des Italiens was as successful as the London one had been, and Champollion himself visited it to copy a number of the texts.

Etched by A. Aglio, after a Drawing by G. Belzoni.

TOMB of SAMETHIS in THEBES.

The flamboyant Drovettis, Salts, Belzonis and Rifauds were not the only Europeans involved in this lucrative trade. Others less well known, more discreet in their activities, but no less effective, bought from the Arabs who disregarded the *firmans* and dug and collected in secret. They were responsible for building collections of papyri which were as important for Egyptology as the monuments sold to the big museums.

Finally, there were those who visited Egypt purely for interest's sake. Their descriptions and drawings of those same monuments, temples and tombs that were in the process of being robbed provided Egyptologists back home with invaluable evidence.

The looting of antiquities in the early 19th century was nothing short of scandalous, but if it destroyed a great deal, it also salvaged much else. Between 1820 and 1828 thirteen entire temples disappeared, their stones either used to build factories or ending up in lime kilns; and no one will ever know how many statues and reliefs suffered the same fate. The objects that were pillaged, on the other hand, were at least preserved for posterity.

The paintings and drawings by the Scotsman David Roberts (1796-1864) during his stay in the Nile valley provide excellent evidence of the state of Egyptian and Nubian monuments in 1838 and 1839, capturing *in situ* the colours that have long since faded. Above: Part of the Ptolemaic temple of Kom Ombo, north of Aswan. Right: entrance of the temple of Hathor at Dendera still only partially dug out.

Illustration from the *Panorama of Egypt and Nubia,* published in 1838 by the French architect Hector Horeau, showing (without any regard for distances) the principal monuments of Egypt, from Pompey's Pillar at Alexandria (bottom centre) to Philae (top), via the Giza pyramids, Karnak and Edfu.

By 1820, thanks to the accounts of travellers, the impressions of painters and the work carried out by the scholars on Napoleon's expedition, the number of recorded Egyptian monuments had considerably increased. Numerous architectural fragments, statues, artefacts and written documents, the papyri, or casts made from reliefs, had been brought back to Europe. The time had come to let them tell their story, and bring ancient Egypt to life.

CHAPTER 5

THE ERA OF THE SCHOLARS

When Champollion (opposite) saw the Great Temple at Abu Simbel, the colours on the reliefs still had their original brilliance, as demonstrated (right) by this figure of Ramesses II offering homage to the gods.

There was, however, one major obstacle to this process: the hieroglyphic texts could not be understood. All the inscriptions on reliefs and wallpaintings were totally mysterious, and this led to repeated mistakes, particularly in attempts to date temples and monuments.

A proper knowledge of ancient Egypt depended on unravelling the texts: the Rosetta Stone provided the key

In August 1799, while inspecting earthworks during the construction of Fort Julien, near Rosetta, an officer of engineers, Pierre Bouchard, caught sight of a black stone covered with inscriptions in an old wall his men were in the process of demolishing. He reported it to his superior, General Menou, who gave the order for the stone to be transported to Alexandria. On examination, it turned out to be a stele comprising three sections in different texts: the topmost in hieroglyphics; the central one in a cursive script that looked something like Arabic; and the bottom one in Greek. The Classical scholars on the expedition translated the latter, which was the copy of a decree by Ptolemy V (196 BC). It seemed likely that the Greek text was a translation of the first two and could therefore provide the key to the hieroglyphic script. This turned out in fact to be the case.

When the French troops capitulated, the scholars planned to secrete the Rosetta Stone on a ship bound for France, but General Tomkins Turner was sent with a military detachment to seize it. Today the Stone stands at the entrance to the Egyptian section in the British Museum in London.

Recognizing the Stone's importance, the French scholars took the opportunity to make

A meeting at the Institut d'Egypte: the entry of Napoleon (centre). General Caffarelli (left) has a wooden leg.

Ruins of Memphis (opposite) in 1798 from the *Description of Egypt*. The pyramids of Giza can be seen in the distance; in the foreground the hand of a colossal statue is being measured and shifted on to planks ready for transportation.

casts and copies of it before releasing it from their care. One such copy fell into the hands of a certain Captain Champoléon, who showed it to his twelve-year-old cousin, Jean-François Champollion.

Champollion was fascinated by the strange hieroglyphic symbols and determined to decipher them. He was to dedicate his whole life to Egypt and its history

Jean-François Champollion was born at Figeac in 1790. His elder brother Jacques-Joseph, later known by the name of Champollion-Figeac, took charge of his early education himself, making him read all the books he could lay his hands on, regardless of subject matter. Then, using his influence as private secretary to Fourier, prefect of Isère, he obtained a grant for the twelve-year-old Jean-François to attend the lycée at Grenoble. Fourier, now secretary of the Institut d'Egypte, had been a member of Napoleon's expedition and directed the two missions despatched to Upper Egypt. Although he had failed to get on the expedition, Champollion-Figeac was also a great Egypt enthusiast. The environment in which Jean-François was brought up thus nourished his ambition to be the first to decipher Egyptian hieroglyphics.

    While a student in Grenoble, he was selective in his studies. He refused to do arithmetic, for example, while supplementing his Latin and Greek (which were compulsory) with Hebrew, Arabic, Syriac and Chaldean (or Aramaic) – all at the age of thirteen! This dedication to studying oriental languages was focused on a precise goal: Egypt. The Bible, in its Hebrew and its Greek Septuagint versions, was one of the main sources on the history of ancient Egypt. Syriac and Aramaic formed part of the biblical tradition, while Arabic was spoken by the inhabitants of the Nile valley, and the memory of ancient Egypt was perpetuated in the work of Arabic geographers and historians.

Portrait of Champollion.

In 1807, at the age of seventeen, Jean-François was sent to Paris, where for the next two years he studied Persian and, most importantly, Coptic. He became quite obsessed with Coptic, convinced that it was in fact ancient Egyptian written in the Greek alphabet.

He wrote to his brother: 'My Coptic is coming along nicely and gives me tremendous pleasure.... I am so very much a Copt that, just for the fun of it, I translate everything that comes into my head into Coptic.... I want to be as conversant in Egyptian as in my own French because Egyptian will be the basis for my great work on the papyri.' He had said it at last: 'my great work' – deciphering hieroglyphs. He was eighteen at the time.

Back in Grenoble, Jean-François obtained his doctorate and was appointed secretary of the Faculty of Letters, then, at nineteen, assistant professor of ancient history. He began his first great work (its lengthy title typical of the time): *Egypt under the Pharaohs or Research into the Geography, Religion, Language, Writing and History of Egypt before the Invasion of Cambyses.* It was a huge project and he only ever finished the first section, on geography (published in 1814).

At twenty-four, he was just beginning to make a name for himself, when his career came to an abrupt halt. Grenoble was one of the first towns to rally to Napoleon's cause after he left Elba, and it was rumoured that it was Jean-François Champollion who climbed the citadel and took down the Bourbons' white flag. The

"On Monday, at a quarter past eight, I leave for the Collège de France, where I arrive at nine.... I attend M. de Sacy's Persian class until ten. Since Hebrew, Syriac and Chaldean begins at mid-day, I go straight from Persian to M. Audran's.... We spend the next two hours chatting about oriental languages and translating some Hebrew, Syrian, Chaldean or Arabic, and we always set aside half an hour for Chaldean and Syriac grammar. At noon, we go down and he gives his Hebrew class. He calls me the patriarch because I am his best student. On leaving class at one, I travel across Paris to the Ecole Spéciale, where, at two o'clock, I go to M. Langlès's class. M. Langlès devotes some extra time to me in the evenings."
Paris, 26 December 1807

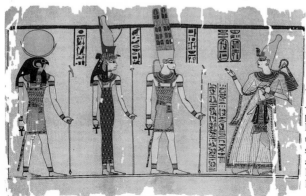

Except for the *Book of the Dead,* illustrated papyri are rare. The large Harris Papyrus (left), in the British Museum, shows Ramesses III addressing the gods of Karnak: Amun, Mut and Khonsu.

two brothers were presented to Napoleon, who encouraged Jean-François to publish his recently completed *Coptic Dictionary.* This blatant rallying to the imperial cause did not impress Louis XVIII, who removed both brothers from office after the Battle of Waterloo. Exiled to Figeac, they opened a private school, where they experimented with the new educational methods being imported from England. It was not a pursuit calculated to advance the decipherment of hieroglyphs.

Thanks to the intervention of friends in Paris, Jean-François was reinstated at Grenoble in 1818 – but only for a short time. In 1821 disturbances broke out in the town, and Jean-François' involvement in them led once more to the loss of his job.

He fled to Paris, where he stayed with his brother, who was now private secretary to Dacier, a Hellenist and permanent secretary of the Académie des Inscriptions et Belles-Lettres. His exile in Paris enabled Jean-François

Page of a hieratic papyrus (left) similar to the ones Champollion deciphered in Turin in 1824.

Wall painting from Abu Simbel from Champollion, *Monuments of Egypt and Nubia.* It shows Ramesses II in his chariot heading a procession of prisoners-of-war captured in 'the land of Kush' (Sudan). A soldier precedes the pharaoh's horse, while his pet leopard runs alongside.

to devote himself to research and consult documents to which he had had no previous access.

Rivals in the decipherment race

In the race to decipher Egyptian hieroglyphs, Champollion had three rivals: his fellow countryman Baron Antoine Isaac Silvestre de Sacy (1758-1838), the Englishman Dr Thomas Young (1773-1829) and the Swede Johan David Åkerblad (1763-1819). Of the three, Thomas Young posed the biggest threat. Like Champollion, he was a child prodigy: at fourteen, he already knew Greek, Latin, French, Italian, Hebrew, Aramaic, Syriac, Arabic, Persian, Turkish and Ethiopian! But unlike Champollion, he had no single overriding passion. While he was continuing his linguistic studies, he trained as a doctor and went into medical practice in London. He studied botany and developed an interest in physics, later becoming famous for his wave theory of light.

Young, Åkerblad, de Sacy and Champollion each possessed a copy of the Rosetta Stone texts and it was upon these that their inquiries were based. At first sight, the problem seemed simple: the existence of a known text – the Greek one – meant that it should be possible to locate and determine the nature of the corresponding words in the hieroglyphic and demotic versions. And yet, twenty years after the Stone's discovery, none of the four experts had made any real headway. In 1802 Åkerblad and de Sacy were both able to decipher a few words of the demotic version, and in 1819 Young correctly interpreted a dozen or so words, while misinterpreting a number of others.

Champollion kept a watchful eye on his rivals' activities, anxious lest they should steal a march on him. This professional rivalry often made him unjust: he described Young's discoveries as 'mere bragging' and declared that Åkerblad could not even read 'three words of an Egyptian inscription'.

Despite his jibes, in 1820 Champollion himself was scarcely any further advanced than they were. There was a fundamental question which none of them had been able to answer. Was the Egyptian script ideographic; in other words, did each sign correspond to an idea? Or was it phonetic, with each sign representing a sound?

Thomas Young endeavoured to translate the Rosetta Stone in 1819, placing the demotic and hieroglyphic texts one above the other, so that he could compare them line by line.

Abu Simbel, painted profile of one of the Syrian prisoners.

Finally, on 14 September 1822, Champollion concluded that Egyptian was partly ideographic and partly phonetic. (For a detailed account of his methods and results see pp. 3-9.) Now that he had made this discovery, his one concern was to apply it as widely as possible. He read as many texts as he could lay his hands on, going to Turin, where the Drovetti Collection was now on view, and Aix, where he deciphered the papyri Sallier had just bought. At Livorno, he saw the Salt Collection, which he persuaded Charles X to buy. The king appointed him conservator of the Egyptian Collections in the Louvre, but he scarcely took the time to fulfil such duties as the post entailed.

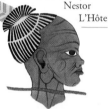

Frontispiece and head of an African prisoner from *Monuments of Egypt and Nubia*. Below: The camp at Philae, watercolour by Nestor L'Hôte

On 31 July 1828 Champollion realized his dream: he set sail for Egypt

In the company of experienced illustrators like Nestor L'Hôte (1804-42) and Pierre Lehoux, a pupil of Gros, as well as an Italian team led by his pupil and friend Ippolito Rosellini (1800-43), Champollion spent fifteen months travelling through Egypt, from Alexandria to Aswan. He visited Nubia, going as far as the Second Cataract, and spent fifteen days in Abu

Simbel. Everywhere he went he read, translated and copied texts. From Wadi Halfa (1 January), he sent greetings to Dacier, the permanent secretary of the Académie, adding: 'Now that I have followed the course of the Nile from its mouth to the Second Cataract, I am in a position to tell you that we need change nothing in our *Letter on the Alphabet of the Hieroglyphs*; our alphabet is correct: it applies equally well to the Egyptian monuments built during the time of the Romans and the Ptolemies and – what is of much greater interest – to the inscriptions in all the temples, palaces and tombs dating from the time of the pharaohs.' Champollion's great work, *Monuments of Egypt and Nubia,* was not published until 1845, thirteen years after his death.

Wall paintings at Abu Simbel (above and below). In a letter from Abu Simbel, Champollion mentions 'Two lines of African prisoners, one of them Negroes, the other barbarians. These groups are perfectly drawn, eye-catching and wonderfully animated.'

Lepsius and Wilkinson gave the impetus to Egyptology in Germany and England

Karl Richard Lepsius (1810-84), a German from Saxony, went to Paris in 1833, attended Letronne's lectures at the Collège de France and learnt to read hieroglyphs from Champollion's posthumous works.

After four years spent inspecting the Egyptian collections in England, Italy and the Netherlands and perfecting his knowledge of Egyptian, Lepsius led the expedition to Egypt (1842-45) organized by the king of Prussia in imitation of Champollion's. On his return to Germany, he was appointed professor at the University of Berlin and published the twelve volumes of his *Discoveries in Egypt and Ethiopia*, complete with 894 large-format (55 x 70 cm) illustrations. Along with the *Description of Egypt* and Champollion's *Monuments of Egypt and Nubia*, Lepsius' *Discoveries in Egypt and Ethiopia* continues to be a standard reference work for Egyptologists today.

Sir John Gardner Wilkinson (1797-1875), who was only a few years younger than Champollion, may be regarded as the founder of Egyptology in England. He went to Egypt in 1821 and remained there for twelve years, carrying out numerous excavations in the Theban area. His great work, *The Manners and Customs of the*

Wilkinson found this mummy's head during excavations at Thebes and immediately produced a watercolour of it – the equivalent of photographing it today.

Ancient Egyptians (1837), reproduces his copies of ancient texts and his drawings and was the first and, for a long time, the only work to describe the daily life of peasants and artisans during the time of the pharaohs.

Prisse d'Avennes went to Egypt as engineer and hydrographer

The Frenchman Achille Prisse d'Avennes (1807-79) was something of an eccentric. After studying engineering and architecture, he fought on the Greek side in the Morean war in 1826, acted as secretary to the governor-general of the Indies, and then left for Palestine and later Egypt. He worked for Mohammed Ali as a civil engineer and hydrographer in 1829, and was appointed professor of topography at the Egyptian army's General Staff School. He was easily offended and fell out with the school's director, and was transferred to the infantry school in Damietta as 'professor of fortifications'. Here

The mortuary temple of Seti I at Thebes, on the west bank of the Nile, drawn by Lepsius in 1844. The fields are partially flooded and the Colossi of Memnon (far background, left) are standing in water.

he had an opportunity to explore the ancient monuments in the Nile Delta, while perfecting his Arabic and learning to read hieroglyphs. In 1836 he resigned from his post, changed his name to Edriss-Effendi and began wearing Turkish clothes. From now on he was to devote his time entirely to archaeology.

In 1838, following a trip to Nubia and Abu Simbel, Prisse settled down in Luxor, where he owned a magnificent house and boat, from which he flew the Union Jack. He claimed, in fact, that he was a descendant of the Princes of Aven and Carnarvon, a Welsh family who had taken refuge in France during the time of Cromwell! He seems nevertheless to have had the interests of France at heart.

Archaeology as patriotism: the rivalry of Prisse d'Avennes and Lepsius.

When he discovered that Lepsius intended to remove the Royal Chamber or Hall of Ancestors from the temple at Karnak, Prisse recruited a team of men to cut the stone blocks into sections, to box them up and to set off with them for Cairo.

En route he passed the Prussian flotilla and invited Lepsius on board. One of those present at the time describes what followed: 'The German doctor told Prisse d'Avennes that he had come to Egypt with the express purpose of fetching Tuthmosis III's Hall of Ancestors for the Berlin Museum. Prisse refrained from mentioning that the Royal Chamber's entire collection of reliefs was inside the boxes on which they were, at that very moment, sitting drinking coffee.'

Prisse offered France Karnak's Hall of Ancestors (today in the Louvre) and also a very long papyrus he had bought from a man from Gourna. The Prisse Papyrus, which is housed in the Bibliothèque Nationale, claims to be the oldest book in the world: it dates to 2000 BC and is a copy of an even older text attributed to a certain Ptahhotep, an official in the service of a pharaoh living in *c.* 2450 BC.

During his lengthy stay in Egypt – almost twenty years – Prisse d'Avennes amassed a considerable quantity of notes, plans, sketches, drawings and prints, which provided the raw material for his *History of Egyptian Monumental Art, from Ancient Times to Roman Rule.*

Painting of two thrones from the tomb of Ramesses III, in the Valley of the Kings from Prisse d'Avennes, *History of Egyptian Monumental Art.*

Lithograph of the Hypostyle Hall of the temple at Esna, produced by Lepsius in 1843. At the time only the hall was accessible; the temple was still largely buried under debris, as can be seen from the rubble-strewn stairway leading down into the hypostyle.

Auguste Mariette (1821-81) did as much for Egyptian archaeology as Champollion had done for Egyptian hieroglyphs. It was Mariette who, under the aegis of the viceroy Saïd Pasha, founded the Egyptian Antiquities Service and thereby put a stop to the systematic pillaging of ancient monuments. By gathering the fruits of the service's excavations in the little museum he set up in the Cairo suburb of Bulaq, Mariette was the founder of the present Cairo Museum.

CHAPTER 6

ARCHAEOLOGISTS TO THE RESCUE

This Apis Bull statue, now in the Louvre, once stood at the entrance to the Serapeum at Memphis.

The Empress Eugénie (opposite) visiting the pyramids. She was just one of many visitors to benefit from Mariette's tours.

In 1842 Mariette, a teacher at the Collège de Boulogne, was asked to sort through the papers and notes belonging to his recently deceased cousin, Nestor L'Hôte. At the sight of the wonderful drawings L'Hôte had done as draughtsman to Champollion, Mariette felt a sudden overwhelming attraction for Egypt.

He was later to say of the hieroglyphic symbol representing a duck: 'The Egyptian duck is a dangerous animal: one snap of its beak and you are infected with Egyptology for life.' Meanwhile, he was still in Boulogne, classifying the little collection of Egyptiana at the local museum, which included a sarcophagus covered in inscriptions brought back by Vivant Denon. Not

Some of Nestor L'Hôte's numerous illustrations, like this watercolour of Karnak (in the Louvre), are still unpublished, despite Mariette's efforts to classify them.

understanding hieroglyphs, Denon had rendered the majority of the texts simply as he imagined them. Ignorant of this fact, and himself a novice where hieroglyphs were concerned, Mariette persisted for months in trying to decipher the texts ... without making any sense of them whatsoever! He almost gave up his studies, which he had been pursuing solely with the help of Champollion's *Grammar* and *Dictionary*.

He persevered, however, and began a correspondence with Charles Lenormant and Emmanuel de Rougé, Champollion's successors to the chair of Egyptology at the Collège de France. Both men were astounded at the knowledge Mariette had managed to acquire through his solitary studies. It seems moreover that the Egyptian duck had bitten him fatally: though married, with a family to support, Mariette decided to give up the security of his job in Boulogne and devote himself singlemindedly to the Egyptian venture. Friends in Paris found him a modest position at the Louvre, which involved making labels for the exhibits, and brought in a mere 166 francs 66 centimes (about £16) a month, but it enabled Mariette to continue his studies and to learn Coptic.

In 1850 Mariette received a commission to buy Coptic manuscripts in Egypt

Excavations at Memphis, c. 1859: entrance to the Serapeum.

The timing was unfortunate. Shortly before Mariette's planned visit, two Englishmen had gone to the Coptic monasteries in the Wadi Natrun, got the monks drunk and obtained a large number of manuscripts for nothing. The Coptic patriarch was furious and not inclined to allow any more foreigners access to the monasteries. When Mariette arrived, in October 1850, he met therefore with a point-blank refusal.

Deprived of a job, Mariette decided to abandon his original mission and to use the funds that had been entrusted to him for something quite different. The decision was in character: he was a quick thinker, a man of great self-confidence and initiative, always ready to take risks.

The Bulls of Apis

At Saqqara, on 27 October 1850, Mariette discovered a sphinx half buried in the sand. 'Just at that moment,' he writes, 'a passage from Strabo flashed through my mind: "There is also a Serapeum at Memphis, in a place so very sandy that dunes of sand are heaped up by the winds; and by these some of the sphinxes which I saw were buried even to the head and others were half-visible; from which one might guess the danger if a sand-storm should fall upon a man travelling on foot towards the temple."' And Mariette continues: 'It almost seems as if Strabo wrote that – more than eight centuries ago – precisely as a way of helping us find the famous temple to Serapis. Indeed, there could be no doubt about it: that buried sphinx, the companion to fifteen others I had seen in Alexandria and in Cairo, clearly formed part of an avenue leading to the Serapeum at Memphis! In that instant, I forgot my mission, forgot the patriarch, the monasteries, the Coptic and Syriac manuscripts. And so, 1 November 1850 dawned, bringing with it one of the most beautiful sunrises I have ever seen in Egypt, and thirty-odd workmen assembled, by my orders, near that sphinx which would so radically alter the conditions of my stay in Egypt.'

The Memphis Serapeum, the underground burial chambers of the Apis Bulls, remains one of the great discoveries of Egyptology, ranking alongside those of the royal mummies at Deir el-Bahari, the tomb of Tutankhamun and the royal tombs at Tanis.

Excavations continued for more than two years. The avenue leading to the temple had to be cleared sphinx by sphinx, and Mariette did not reach the Serapeum until 11 February 1851, by which time his resources were virtually exhausted. He had kept quiet about his discovery, but was

"The Serapeum excavations had aroused all my dormant fighting instincts. Back in France, I tried to battle with some text or other, to convince myself that this was what science was all about; but I could not. . . . I began thinking about a new project at Thebes and in the necropolis at Abydos, or drafting a dissertation on the scientific value of setting up a protection service for ancient monuments (one which I would, of course, direct). I would have died or gone mad if there had not been an opportunity for me to return to Egypt more or less immediately."

Mariette
Letter to Maspero

now forced to make an official announcement in France in order to attract further funds. On 26 August 1851 the French parliament, approached by the Institut d'Egypte, voted to award him a phenomenal 30,000 francs to continue his excavations.

In his eagerness Mariette had forgotten one thing: that he was actually in Egypt, and that his finds did not belong to France at all! The Egyptian reaction was prompt: he was ordered to abandon excavations immediately and to hand over to the Egyptian agents any finds he had made so far. Lengthy discussions now ensued between the two countries, and Mariette – in the company of his family, who had grown tired of waiting for him in Paris and sailed out to join him – was obliged to await their outcome. At last, on 12 February 1852, thanks to the mediation of the consul-general of France, the interdict was lifted, and a *firman* officially authorized the French to continue with their excavations.

These were far from easy. When the order to abandon work came, Mariette had just discovered an entrance to the underground chambers containing the mummified bodies of the bulls. Passageways and chambers were in a state of complete disarray: sarcophagus lids had been tipped up and smashed, stelae had been prised from the walls, funerary statuettes and small objects lay scattered on the ground. But thanks to Mariette's efforts, order was finally restored, and the Serapeum became a tourist attraction for important visitors to Egypt.

The discovery of the Serapeum was as important for Mariette personally as it was for Egyptology in general. In February 1851 no one had heard of him; three months later he had an international reputation. Prior to the discovery of the Serapeum he could have settled down to being a librarian or a museum curator; after it such a career would have been unthinkable: now he knew the delights of fieldwork, the sheer intoxication of archaeological discovery, he could no longer live without them.

With the help of Ferdinand de Lesseps (1805-94), who was to construct the Suez Canal between 1859 and 1869, Mariette returned to Egypt in October 1857. He had been given the job of preparing an Egyptian expedition for Prince Napoleon (Napoleon III's cousin), and of assembling a collection of antiquities for the new viceroy,

Whenever an important visitor came to Saqqara, Mariette would first receive them at his own home, then take them personally to the catacombs. Meanwhile, following a carefully rehearsed routine, hundreds of children had been positioned along the length of the main gallery, each sitting motionless on the ground and holding a lighted candle. As one visitor said: 'It is impossible to imagine the impression created by this vast underground passageway, whose lighting, so arranged, has a strange, dreamlike quality.... Leading off the gallery are lateral chambers housing the immense sarcophagi of the Apis Bulls. Each of these was lit up too ... whichever way you turn, the effect is truly magical.' The visit continued with a closer look at the sarcophagi containing the sacred bulls. Three metres high, two metres wide and four metres long, they were carved out of a single granite block, its surface mirror-smooth. A ladder was placed against the end sarcophagus, and on reaching the top, the visitor found inside it a table laid with a silver salver, chased silver goblets and bottles of champagne, the whole lit by candelabra, while ten folding chairs stood by, awaiting the guests.

Saïd Pasha, to present to the prince. Mariette received a warm welcome from Saïd, who gave him money and a steamboat for his use, and he began excavations at once: at Giza, Saqqara, Abydos, Thebes and Elephantine. Prince Napoleon abandoned his projected trip; but, thanks to Saïd Pasha, Mariette was able to fulfil a lifetime ambition.

Mariette in command

On 1 June 1858 Mariette was appointed 'Maamour', Director of the Egyptian Antiquities Service. The viceroy Saïd Pasha gave him full powers and all the resources he required. He had a steamboat to take him from one site to another; authority to recruit all the manpower he needed; and funds to enable him 'to clear and restore the temple ruins, to collect stelae, statues, amulets and any easily transportable objects wherever these were to be found, in order to secure them against the greed of the local peasants or the covetousness of Europeans'.

Mariette had set up the Cairo Museum and established what was to become known as the Antiquities Service. But he had the greatest difficulty in applying the protective measures proposed by that service. There were too many vested interests at stake for the pillaging to cease overnight. Aware now of the value of objects they had

Portrait of Saïd Pasha (1822-63), viceroy of Egypt.

Photo of Mariette with his daughters Louise and Sophie and friends; on the left, the Egyptologist the Marquis de Rochemonteix.

once disregarded, Egyptian peasants continued their excavations in secret.

The cache of royal mummies at Deir el-Bahari

At Thebes, in 1857 and 1858, on the west bank of the Nile, opposite Luxor, Mariette discovered the mummy of Queen Aahotep dating from the 17th dynasty (*c.* 1600 BC) with some very beautiful gold and silver jewelry.

Following an incident involving the governor of the province, the entire population of Gourna learnt that riches of (to them) incalculable value lay beneath the very ground on which they trod. The village was, in fact, built over a cemetery, and many of the villagers' homes were actually situated in tomb chapels hewn out of the rock. These chapels communicated via a series of shafts with the underground chambers where the mummies and burial goods were housed. Following the archaeologists' example, the inhabitants of Gourna were to become the most active clandestine excavators in the whole of Egypt.

From 1875 Luxor dealers began selling a variety of beautiful artefacts, in particular some excellently conserved papyri. A Scottish colonel by the name of Campbell bought a large papyrus in hieratic script which had belonged to the pharaoh Pinedjem (21st dynasty, *c.* 1000 BC); and the name of that same pharaoh was

Photo, taken on 8 May 1882, showing teams of workmen positioning Mariette's marble tomb (a copy of an Old Kingdom sarcophagus) in the garden at Bulaq. The museum that Mariette founded at Bulaq was housed in an old warehouse on the bank of the Nile. Visitors were received in the garden, among the sphinxes and the monumental statues, by the museum's guard dog Bargout and by Mariette's favourite gazelle Finette.

inscribed on the small blue statuettes, or ushabtis, which were also on sale at the time.

Sir Gaston Maspero (1846-1916) heard about the Pinedjem papyrus and guessed it must have come from

Temple of Hatshepsut, Deir el-Bahari. It was at the foot of the cliff near the temple that – after two millennia – the mummies of some of the most famous pharaohs were discovered in 1881.

an unknown tomb. The appearance of the ushabtis led him to suspect that this tomb had recently been robbed.

In the spring of 1881, having succeeded Mariette as director of the Antiquities Service, Maspero began making inquiries in Luxor. These led him to a certain Mustafa Agha Ayat, a dealer in antiquities, but also consular agent for Great Britain, Belgium and Russia – who therefore enjoyed diplomatic immunity. But Mustafa was only the receiver of the stolen goods, and not the person responsible for the actual excavations.

Maspero then narrowed down his inquiries to three inhabitants of Gourna, the Abd el-Rassul brothers. One of them, Mohammed, was employed by Mustafa; the other two were dealers. Maspero had Mohammed arrested and imprisoned in Qena; but he denied any part in the clandestine excavations, and prominent members of the village community vouched for his integrity. So he had to be released. But his stay in prison had given Mohammed time to reflect. Fearing that his brothers might make a scapegoat of him in the wake of some family quarrel, he confessed to the governor that, in 1871, the three of them had indeed discovered a cache of mummies along with various burial goods. Since

The ancient Egyptians believed that these statuettes (above), known as ushabtis or shawabtis, or simply 'answerers', would carry out whatever tasks Osiris, god of the dead, imposed on their owner in the life hereafter. The figures were numerous, since one was required for each day of the year, along with a *reis* (overseer) for every group of ten (thus more than 400 in total); they were placed in wooden ushabti boxes in the tomb, near the coffin. When ushabtis appeared on the antique market, it was a sign (and the same is still true today), that the tomb they belonged to had been found.

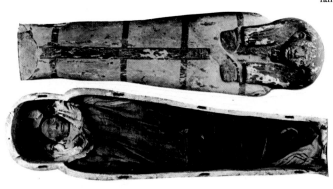

Maspero was in France at the time, the viceroy appointed a commission of inquiry comprising the German Emil Brugsch (Mariette's one-time assistant), the Egyptian curator of the museum at Bulaq and an inspector. On 5 July Mohammed Abd el-Rassul took the three men to the foot of a cliff near the temple of Deir el-Bahari. After a difficult ascent of some sixty metres, they reached a crevice in the rock face. This turned out to be the opening – carefully concealed by sand and stones – of a shaft leading down into the mountainside.

Secrets of the burial chamber

A long passageway led to a large, dimly lit chamber of irregular shape. Brugsch stumbled against the sarcophagi and the funerary goods littering both passageway and chamber. Inscribed on the coffins he passed, he was able to make out by the faint light of his candle the names of the most famous pharaohs of the 18th and 19th dynasties – Amosis I, Tuthmosis I, II and III, Amenophis I, Seti I, Ramesses II and III – and those of some of their queens – Ahmose-Nefertari, Isiemkheb, Maatkare – and of the princes and princesses, their children, and of some major court officials. Brugsch could hardly

Mummy wrapped in reeds, Thebes, 21st dynasty (left).

Gaston Maspero, Mariette's successor at the museum at Bulaq. Sites of his excavations included the pyramids of Giza and the temple at Luxor.

From Deir el-Bahari, the coffin and mummified body of the priest Nebseni (left). 'A gentle little smile still hovered on his lips, and a faint light seemed to gleam from beneath his half-shut lids, while his lashes looked wet and shiny: it was the reflection of the white porcelain eyes that had been placed in the sockets during the embalming.'
Maspero

believe his eyes. In the midst of all these sarcophagi which he had difficulty counting, lay scattered a whole range of burial goods: ushabti boxes, canopic jars in alabaster and limestone (in which the entrails of embalmed bodies were placed), bronze and earthenware jars, writing tablets, and even an entire funerary tent, part of the paraphernalia of a burial. It was from this incredible pile of priceless objects that, for years past, the Abd el-Rassul brothers had been stealing pieces.

The commission was in an awkward position. Now that they had made this extraordinary discovery, what were they to do? Close up the shaft and wait for Maspero's return? But that would be unwise: indiscretions were not only possible, they were inevitable; and how could even an armed guard resist a frenzied crowd drawn here by the piles of accumulated treasures which, in its imagination, it had magnified out of all proportion? Brugsch therefore decided to remove the entire cache and take it straight to Cairo. He recruited three hundred workmen, and in six days sarcophagi, mummies and other items had all been transported to Luxor, and shortly after transferred to a steamboat specially commissioned from Cairo, which 'no sooner loaded, left again for Bulaq with its royal cargo. At which point an odd thing happened. From Luxor to Quft, on both banks of the Nile, dishevelled peasant women followed the boat howling like animals and the men fired shots in the way that they do at a funeral' (Maspero). What were they mourning? Their distant ancestors or the loss of a priceless treasure?

Why had all these mummies been removed from their original tombs and concealed at Deir el-Bahari?

In the 21st dynasty, between *c.* 1150 and *c.* 1080 BC, the inhabitants of Thebes began breaking into the cemeteries and plundering the graves, in particular the royal ones, which they knew to be richly furnished. In spite of the severe penalties such activities incurred – death,

"The Arabs had uncovered a whole vault full of kings. And what kings! The most famous, perhaps, in the entire history of Egypt: Tuthmosis III and Seti I, Amosis the Liberator and Ramesses II the Great.... Emil Brugsch thought he must be hallucinating. And when I see, and touch, the bodies of so many illustrious persons we never imagined could be more than names to us, I too still find it hard to believe that I am not dreaming."

Maspero

amputation of nose and ears or, at the very least, caning of the soles of the feet – the looting continued. It became so widespread in fact that the priests decided to move all the mummies to a single tomb where it would be easier to keep watch over them. After two such moves, the mummies were finally secreted in the great chamber and passageway at Deir el-Bahari, hidden in a mountain.

Thanks to the papyri and material evidence that has come down to us today, it is easy to understand why, given the number of mummies concealed there, the Deir el-Bahari cache contained relatively few funerary goods and virtually no gold or silver, though these were widely used in traditional royal burials. When the priests moved the mummies, the gold and silver had long since been stolen and melted down by the tomb robbers.

Although the priests of the 21st dynasty failed to save many of the funerary goods, they preserved what to them was the essential thing: the royal bodies themselves – the mummies of the greatest pharaohs of the New Kingdom. These, together with the papyri and the texts inscribed on mummies and coffins, provided early Egyptologists with a vast mine of information that Maspero put to good use.

Sarcophagus and mummy (opposite) of the Princess Isiemkheb (21st dynasty, c. 1000 BC), discovered at Deir el-Bahari.

Mummy of Ramesses II (1279-1212 BC), found in the first or royal cache at Deir el-Bahari (below). The discovery of this cache was followed by two other similar finds, one of which (also at Deir el-Bahari) contained the mummies of the high priests and priestesses of Amun. It was Mohammed Abd el-Rassul, one-time-thief-turned-collaborator, who revealed its whereabouts. Not only was Mohammed not prosecuted for the thefts of 1871-81, he actually received a reward of £500 and was put in charge of the cemetery guard at Thebes.

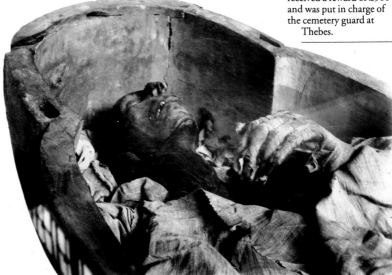

If the discovery of the royal cache at Deir el-Bahari was the stuff that detective stories are made of, the Tutankhamun find could have provided the theme for a fantasy: an English lord who had an accident, an archaeologist in the grip of an obsession, the discovery of a fabulous treasure, then the revenge, slow and inexorable, as the pharaoh, robbed of his riches, destroys the protagonists of the drama one by one. The reality was rather different, but no less astonishing.

CHAPTER 7
THE REDISCOVERY OF ANCIENT EGYPT

Upper half of Tutankhamun's inner coffin of solid gold, set with semi-precious stones and coloured glass.

Throne in which the young king sat when presiding over religious ceremonies: ebony inlaid with ivory and various gemstones.

We owe the discovery of the tomb of Tutankhamun – so crucial for Egyptology – to a conjunction of three separate circumstances, the first occurring in the 12th century BC, the other two in our own century. In *c.* 1140 BC, while Theban workmen were excavating the great tomb of Ramesses VI and piling the rock spoil close to the entrance, they unintentionally covered up a tiny tomb that had already lain forgotten for two centuries. It was thus thanks to Ramesses VI's workmen that the tomb of Tutankhamun escaped the fate of all the others in the Valley of the Kings.

Excavation of Tutankhamun's tomb in 1923. Attracted by the news in the press, crowds of tourists gathered daily round the perimeter to watch the artefacts being removed from the tomb.

In 1892 a young English artist, Howard Carter (1873-1939), was hired by the Egypt Exploration Fund to draw the reliefs and inscriptions on the temple of Mentuhotep (2060-2010 BC) at Deir el-Bahari. He joined the Antiquities Service in 1899 and was appointed Inspector of Antiquities of Upper Egypt. While at Deir el-Bahari, he had been intrigued by the Valley of the Kings, and was convinced that a number of royal tombs remained undiscovered there. Persuading a wealthy American, Theodore Davis, to apply for the concession to dig, he began excavations in the Valley. Davis put up the money, and Carter himself oversaw and directed the work. It was thus that he discovered the tombs of Queen Hatshepsut and of Tuthmosis IV, both robbed in antiquity. For four years, he continued to explore the Valley of the Kings, familiarizing himself with its every detail. In 1903 a promotion to the post of Inspector of Lower and Middle Egypt obliged him to move nearer to Cairo. The post was short-lived, however. In the course of an argument between the *ghaffirs* (guards) of the Serapeum and a group of tourists, Carter took the *ghaffirs'* side. But the visitors were influential people; they lodged a complaint, and the British consul, anxious to avoid a diplomatic incident, demanded that Carter offer his apologies. Instead, he resigned from his post, setting up home in Cairo, where he earned a living painting landscapes for the tourists.

It was a strange turn for fate to take. Would the tomb of Tutankhamun have been discovered, one wonders, if those awkward visitors had not come and made a scene at the Serapeum? Probably not. Had the incident not occurred, Carter would have stayed on at Saqqara and never met Lord Carnarvon or recommended the Valley of the Kings as a promising site for his excavations.

George Edward Stanhope Molyneux Herbert, 5th Earl of Carnarvon (1866-1923) was the archetypal English aristocrat. Educated at Eton and Trinity College, Cambridge, he was a member of the Jockey Club, a man of substantial means and a collector. He travelled a great deal, but his principal passions in life were breeding racehorses, hunting and cars. Now it was here that fate intervened a third time. During a trip to Germany Carnarvon had a very bad car accident which left him a semi-invalid for life. His lungs were affected and his doctors recommended that he spend his winters in Egypt. This was in 1903, the same year that Carter, having resigned his full-time post, was idling in Cairo.

Lord Carnarvon became attached to Egypt in the course of these regular visits and requested a licence to begin some excavations. Gaston Maspero, the then director of the Egyptian Antiquities Service, saw this as

Howard Carter (above top), who devoted more than ten years of his life to removing the hundreds of items discovered inside the tomb. He died in 1939, before publishing his final report.

Lord Carnarvon (above) financed the project and took an active part in the Tutankhamun excavations. He died from an infected mosquito bite on 5 April 1923 – before the tomb had been fully opened. His death led to the story of the pharaoh's curse.

an opportunity to help Carter, for whom he had the highest regard. It was on his recommendation, therefore, that Lord Carnarvon, whose own knowledge of archaeology was non-existent, hired Carter as his technical adviser and excavator. Carter proposed that they begin their explorations in the Thebes area, in the burial site reserved for the nobility. They continued digging there until 1912. Meanwhile, Davis' licence for the Valley of the Kings had expired and, assuming, like Maspero, that the Valley's resources were now exhausted, he did not bother to renew it. Carter persuaded Carnarvon to take it up and to continue his excavations.

Carter and Carnarvon explored the Valley of the Kings over the next ten years without success. Losing heart at last, they were about to abandon their search....

The flight of steps

On 4 November 1922, the workmen uncovered a flight of stone steps, sixteen in all, leading below ground. These steps, hewn out of the rock, led down to a walled-up entrance whose plaster facing bore the seals of the guardians of the cemetery and those of a little-known pharaoh, Tutankhamun. All of them were intact! Carnarvon was in England at the time. Carter called a halt to the excavations, had the entrance to the tomb covered up again and sent Carnarvon the following telegram: 'At last have made wonderful discovery in Valley; a magnificent tomb with seals intact; re-covered same for your arrival; congratulations.' On 23 November Carnarvon arrived. It took two days to clear the staircase and doorway once more and to unblock the latter. Beyond it was a sloping corridor piled to the ceiling with rubble. This in turn led to another doorway identical to the first, also walled up, and bearing the same seals. By the 26th the rubble had been cleared. With trembling hands, Carter removed a few stones from the second doorway and held a lighted candle to the opening. The warm air from the tomb made the candle flame flicker at first; then strange shapes began to loom out of the darkness – animals and statues – and from all sides came the gleam of gold. Carter could neither move nor speak. Carnarvon, in an agony of suspense, asked: 'Can you see anything?' Still hardly able to believe his eyes, Carter replied: 'Yes, wonderful things.'

Treasures from the tomb. Sculpture of the young king (above) as the sun-god Re emerging from a lotus flower, symbol of rebirth. Gilded wood mirror box (below) in the shape of the symbol of life (*ankh*).

G old-bladed daggers from the tomb (above).

V isible at last: the stone sarcophagus, glittering in the beam of light (left).

The tomb of Tutankhamun, the smallest royal tomb in the Valley of the Kings, was literally stuffed with goods: statues, beds, chairs, models of boats, chariots, weapons, vases, various chests and caskets – all jumbled up in the most indescribable confusion.

Each object had to be removed one at a time. It took the excavators four years to reach the burial chamber.

Carter and Carnarvon open the antechamber

Valley of the Kings (opposite); entrance to Tutankhamun's tomb (A) and beyond it the tomb of Ramesses VI (B

1 Stairs and passage
2 Antechamber
3 Annexe
4 Burial chamber
5 Treasury

The antechamber was stuffed with goods, all still in the chaotic pile left by the looters who broke into the tomb shortly after it was first sealed. Top: Northern part of the antechamber Statues stand guard on either side of the walled up entrance to the buria chamber. Piled on the le are various chests, alabaster vases, chairs an a funeral couch with lion headed side-pieces; on the right, the remains of bunch of flowers. Centr Couch with the head of cow, representing the goddess Hathor, and, piled beneath it, food boxes (largely containin geese and ducks). Left: Southern part of the antechamber, with dismantled royal chariot and a couch with the head of a hippopotamus representing Thoueris.

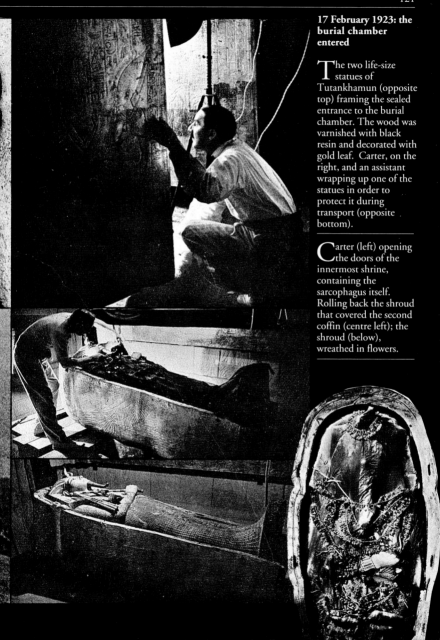

17 February 1923: the burial chamber entered

The two life-size statues of Tutankhamun (opposite top) framing the sealed entrance to the burial chamber. The wood was varnished with black resin and decorated with gold leaf. Carter, on the right, and an assistant wrapping up one of the statues in order to protect it during transport (opposite bottom).

Carter (left) opening the doors of the innermost shrine, containing the sarcophagus itself. Rolling back the shroud that covered the second coffin (centre left); the shroud (below), wreathed in flowers.

255.A.

The King's gold mask (opposite), inside the third and last coffin. Extending down on to the mummy's chest is a collar of beads and flowers; draped round its head, a linen scarf.

The Treasury (left). The jackal Anubis, guardian of the cemetery, is lying on a small pylon, partially blocking the entrance. A linen scarf is draped across his back and knotted at his neck, and the entire structure rests on a portable frame. When the chamber was first opened, a candle was lying at the foot of the statue; it had fallen from a stand on which a magic invocation was inscribed. The large gilded wooden chest behind Anubis housed the alabaster canopic chest containing the small gold canopic coffinettes in which the king's entrails were placed after his embalming.

The young king's sarcophagus was itself enclosed within four huge gilded wooden shrines, each one fitting inside the other and the second one covered with a linen pall decorated with gold rosettes. Within the four shrines stood the king's quartzite sarcophagus. Inside this, three further coffins in the shape of a mummy lay one inside the other, like Russian dolls: the first two were made of gilded wood set with semi-precious gems, the third of solid gold (110.4 kg). The mummy lay within this last coffin, its head and the upper part of its chest and shoulders covered with a mask of solid gold encrusted with semi-precious stones and coloured glass.

In 1939 at Tanis, in the Nile Delta, Pierre Montet discovered several intact royal tombs

Although very unusual, the discovery of an intact royal burial, like Tutankhamun's, was not a unique event in the history of Egyptology. In 1939 the French archaeologist Pierre Montet (1885-1966) was excavating the temple area at Tanis, in the eastern part of the Nile Delta, when he stumbled upon the entrance to a pit.

Pierre Montet holding a large silver stand and dish discovered in King Psousennes' burial chamber. Excavations at Tanis, modern-day San el-Hagar (below).

Once cleared, this revealed the flagged roof of ... a stone-built tomb! The pit itself had been dug by robbers as a means of reaching the tomb. As it turned out, this tomb was one of a group of burial vaults belonging to the pharaohs of the 21st and 22nd dynasties whose capital was at Tanis. The first tomb to be discovered, that of Osorkon II, had been robbed; but King Psousennes' was intact, as were others, nearby, belonging to four other important personages. The burial goods at Tanis included silver coffins, gold masks, jewels and gold, silver, bronze and alabaster vases.

The continuing saga

From 1881, the year of Mariette's death, to our own time the Egypt of the pharaohs was gradually pieced together by experts like Brugsch, Maspero, Montet and others. Each year brought its share of discoveries. More and more sites, in both Egypt and Nubia, were methodically explored. As new documentary material came to light, the philologists, epigraphers and historians were all kept busy. Large volumes of texts began to appear, followed by grammars and dictionaries, and gradually the history of ancient Egypt unfolded before the world's eyes. Egyptology had left its infancy behind and was now maturing into adulthood.

For an excavator like Mariette, Maspero, Carter or Montet, the original discovery marked the beginning of a long and exhausting process, especially in the case of important finds, such as those of the royal burial ground at Tanis, the tomb of Tutankhamun, the Deir el-Bahari cache or the Serapeum. Once a plan of the site had been drawn, along with the precise location of artefacts, the objects had to be removed with care, transferred to the storeroom or laboratory, cleaned, described, drawn, analysed, labelled and restored. It was hardly surprising, therefore, that it took Carter, assisted by numerous experts, more than ten years to clear and pack the contents of Tutankhamun's tomb and move them to the Cairo Museum. Mariette, working single-handed, never actually managed to finish cataloguing the thousands of items discovered at the Serapeum.

The tombs cut into the cliff face at Beni Hasan dated from the 12th dynasty (c. 1900 B.C.). A number were decorated with wall paintings, like this fishing scene below

(tomb no. 3). While Champollion and Wilkinson described the paintings, it was Lepsius who first correctly dated and explained the site.

Tombs cut into the mountainside were thought to be theft-proof. The first drawings (published in the *Description of Egypt*) of the Asyut tombs, also rock-cut, were produced by Vivant Denon in 1798. Gaston Maspero later excavated the site.

• Beni Hasan

•Tell el-Amarna

• Asyut

Sohag

time of
¹ (c. 1200
¹ of the
:ty
ipeum
nal
of the
orshiped

at Memphis. Mariette discovered the catacombs in 1850, and many of the items he found there are in the Louvre today.

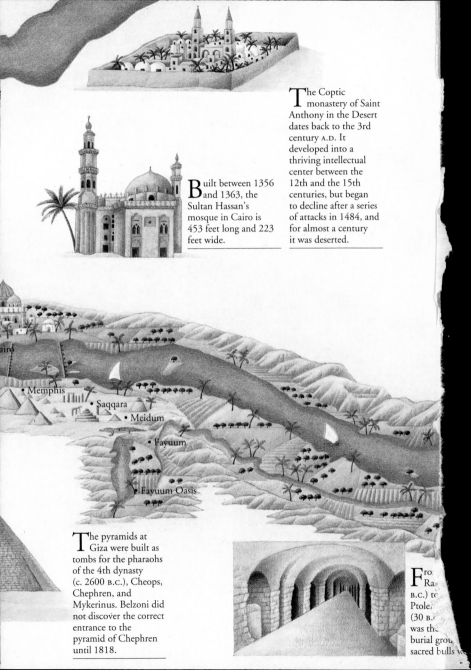

The Coptic monastery of Saint Anthony in the Desert dates back to the 3rd century A.D. It developed into a thriving intellectual center between the 12th and the 15th centuries, but began to decline after a series of attacks in 1484, and for almost a century it was deserted.

Built between 1356 and 1363, the Sultan Hassan's mosque in Cairo is 453 feet long and 223 feet wide.

• Memphis

• Saqqara

• Meidum

• Fayuum

• Fayuum Oasis

The pyramids at Giza were built as tombs for the pharaohs of the 4th dynasty (c. 2600 B.C.), Cheops, Chephren, and Mykerinus. Belzoni did not discover the correct entrance to the pyramid of Chephren until 1818.

Fro...
Ra...
B.C.) t...
Ptole...
(30 B....
was th...
burial grou...
sacred bulls...

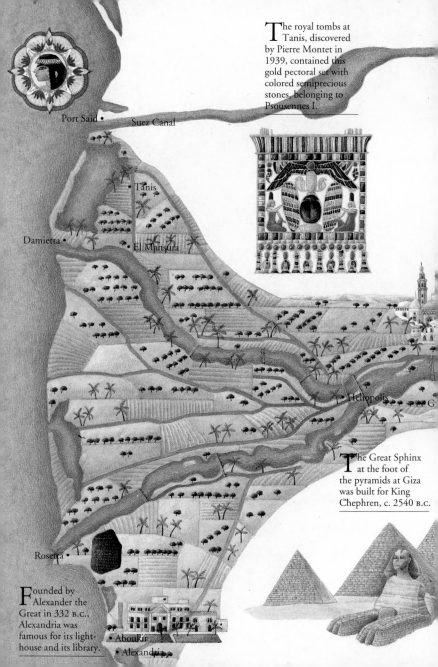

The royal tombs at Tanis, discovered by Pierre Montet in 1939, contained this gold pectoral set with colored semiprecious stones, belonging to Psousennes I.

Port Said •

Suez Canal

• Tanis

Damietta •

• El Mansura

Heliopolis

G

The Great Sphinx at the foot of the pyramids at Giza was built for King Chephren, c. 2540 B.C.

Rosetta •

Founded by Alexander the Great in 332 B.C., Alexandria was famous for its lighthouse and its library.

• Aboukir

• Alexandria

Philae •

Abu Simbel •

• Cairo

• Alexandria

Lake Nasser

• Dendur

Only the Egyptian stretch of the river is shown here. The remotest source of the Nile lies beyond Lake Nasser, a huge reservoir created during the 1960s.

Abu Simbel was the site least known to travelers. It was discovered by Burckhardt in 1813. In 1817 Belzoni cleared the entrance to the Great Temple. The colossal statues flanking the entrance are of Ramses II, who built the temple in the 13th century B.C.

In 1965–72, when the Aswan Dam was built 155 miles downstream, thereby creating Lake Nasser, the two temples at Abu Simbel were dismantled in twenty-ton sections and re-erected nearby on higher ground.

DOCUMENTS

Great moments in the rediscovery of ancient Egypt,
written evidence of travellers and scholars,
past and present

The Egyptian campaign

On 19 May 1798 an army under the command of Napoleon Bonaparte set sail from the port of Toulon. On board, besides the soldiers and the crew, were a party of scientific scholars and artists. Their expedition was to have enormous consequences, not just for the personal career of Napoleon himself but, above all, in terms of the history of archaeology.

There has probably been no expedition more foolhardy in the entire history of France than its conquest of Egypt in 1798. Foolhardy in the sense that this expedition consisted in shipping off the best army in the Republic – without disclosing the ultimate destination – on vessels that risked being either captured or sunk by the English, who had complete naval supremacy in the Mediterranean. Foolhardy because it meant invading – in mid-July too, indicating a total misjudgment of climate – a country against which war had not even been declared. And foolhardy, moreover, since the avowed motive of the expedition was to found a colony, at a time precisely when the right of nations to self-determination was being proclaimed. The ultimate irony, however, was that the French army was to find itself a prisoner in the country it had conquered, unable to return while its general flew back to the aid of the Republic, now threatened by a coalition of its enemies that could long have been foreseen.

And yet, foolhardy or otherwise, the Egyptian expedition had an impact on world affairs. By uncovering the splendours of that 'lost' (or at least mysterious) civilization, it gave rise to the study of ancient Egypt and its language: to Egyptology. And it promoted Egypt's economic growth, its takeoff as we should say in the 20th century, restoring it to a position of importance in the Near East. It is for these reasons that the Egyptian campaign – not, as it happens, Napoleon's most prestigious – continues to fascinate archaeologists and historians today.

After the signing of the peace treaty of Campo Formio (1797) that ended the war between revolutionary France and Austria, Napoleon became the Republic's

Napoleon's army embarks for Egypt, 19 May 1798. The fleet of two hundred ships was soon to be reinforced by a contingent from Italy.

most popular general. And how could a popular general under an unpopular regime fail to capitalize on the situation? Yet, sensitive as he always was to the political situation, he judged a coup to be premature. Having rid itself of all its opponents, the Directoire appeared for the moment invulnerable. Moreover, generals who meddled in politics tended to be regarded with suspicion, as La Fayette, Dumouriez and Pichegru had all discovered to their cost. Napoleon's prestige rested not only on his victories, but on his unswerving loyalty to the Republic. To depart from such loyalty now, or to be seen to do so, would be sheer suicide.

So, he had to wait, while ensuring that he was not forgotten. His election to the Institut, on 25 December 1797, was insufficient to capture public attention for long. What was required was a major expedition. Should he take up the attempt to invade England? That was a hazardous enterprise – Napoleon could not be sure of succeeding where Hoche had already failed. Then, on 3 July 1797, in a public lecture at the Institut, Talleyrand [the French Foreign Minister]

read a paper on the advantages to be gained from the creation of new colonies. During the course of this paper he had referred to Choiseul's project calling for the annexation of Egypt to France. Egypt was fashionable. In 1785 Savary had published his *Letters Written from Egypt*, and it was followed two years later by Volney's *Journey in Syria and Egypt*. Prior to this date, little had been known about this province of the Ottoman Empire, and next to nothing regarding its illustrious past. Why then was Egypt such a worthy target of France's interest? In answer, Talleyrand pointed to the approaching end of Turkish domination in the Near East and Europe, suggesting that France should take advantage of this situation by seizing the spoils the Turks left behind them and protecting its trade with the East....

Talleyrand observed that once Egypt had been taken, an expedition could be sent from Suez to India, where it would join forces with Tipoo-Sahib, Sultan of Mysore since the expulsion of the British in 1784. England would be defenceless against a coastal attack launched in secret. Russia, Prussia and Austria were busy dividing up Poland and could scarcely protest after having wiped the Polish kingdom off the map....

Such an expedition was entirely in line with 18th-century politics. On closer examination though, it seems like an act of pure folly. The conquest of Egypt would deprive France of an army and a general, both of them experienced, precisely at a time when war threatened to break out again at home. And who could foresee the outcome of such an operation? Quite apart from the risk – despite all the fine words – of, at the very least, 'alienating' France's allies the Turks. It was agreed, on this account, that Talleyrand should go to Constantinople and explain to the Sultan that the French initiative was not an act of war; but, for a variety of reasons, the mission never took place.

In the face of all this, there is something wanton in Talleyrand's encouragement of the Napoleonic expedition. According to his brother Joseph – and contrary to popular belief – Napoleon only embarked on the campaign after considerable hesitation and carefully weighing up the risks involved. In the *Memoirs of Fouché* it is said that he regarded the expedition as a trap, and we can be sure that the Directoire would have had few regrets in saying farewell to a general who made his presence at home so forcibly felt. Whatever his reservations, Napoleon prepared speedily for departure and left for Toulon on 4 May 1798. The die was cast.

Preparations for the expedition had taken place in the utmost secrecy in order to evade British surveillance in the Mediterranean. To prevent any possible indiscretion, the soldiers themselves had not been briefed about their mission. Thus it was that Marshal Joachim Murat,

then garrisoned in Italy, received the order to present himself in Milan. Here, he learnt that he was to go to Genoa as quickly as possible, and that he would be commanding the 14th and 18th Dragoons on the 'great expedition', its destination as yet undisclosed. In this manner, preparations were finalized within a month. Had too much time elapsed, British suspicions might have been alerted. The expedition was funded with money taken from Berne at the time of the French intervention. What did cause Napoleon's army genuine amazement was the sight of 21 mathematicians, 3 astronomers, 17 civil engineers, 13 naturalists and mining engineers, 4 architects, 8 draughtsmen, 10 men of letters, and 22 printers armed with Greek, Latin and Arabic founts, all trooping on board. The list of distinguished individuals who were to accompany the expedition was an impressive one and included: the geometrician and physicist Gaspard Monge; the chemist Claude-Louis Berthollet; the scientist Geoffroy Saint-Hilaire; the archaeologist Edmé Jomard; the Orientalist Pierre-Amédée Jaubert; Baron Dominique Vivant Denon (who was in charge of these scholars); Nicolas-Jacques Conté, famous for his crayon-drawings; the poet François-Auguste Parseval-Grandmaison; a painter, and a pianist.

It was not just the best army in the Republic (35,000 men in total) that was to set sail for Egypt, but also its scientific élite. Was Napoleon merely seeking to please the idealists, or to place the expedition in line with the grand 18th-century tradition of scientific voyages? Or was he setting up an alibi in case of defeat? In all events it is easy to imagine the consequences of an interception by Nelson. On 19 May the two hundred

The capture of Alexandria. The French fleet arrived on 1 July 1798. Napoleon sent in three divisions, and the governor and his troops surrendered on 3 July.

vessels under Admiral Brueys' command put out to sea. How, one wonders, did a fleet of this size, with a further reinforcement from Italy, succeed in evading the English? Nelson failed to intercept it on two occasions. En route Napoleon seized Malta, which was to serve the expedition as a temporary base. It was at this point that the troops received official confirmation of their destination. On 1 July the French disembarked at Alexandria, taking the city's inhabitants entirely by surprise. Since the invasion came without warning of any kind, resistance to it was limited.

On 2 July Napoleon made an ingenious announcement to the townspeople, in which he declared: 'For some time, the governors of Egypt, the beys, have showered insults on the French nation, treating its merchants with contempt. The time has now come to punish them.' Napoleon also presented himself in the role of a liberator: 'Where there's a fine piece of land, who does it belong to? The Mamelukes. Where there's a beautiful slave, a beautiful horse, a beautiful house, who does it belong to? The Mamelukes. If Egypt has been leased to the Mamelukes, then let them show us that lease granted them by God. But God is just and compassionate towards the people.' This was why He had elected Napoleon, the champion of equality, to come and liberate the Egyptians. But was Napoleon not an infidel? No, replied Napoleon: 'More than the Mamelukes', he said, 'I respect God, His prophet and the Koran.' And he added: 'Was it not we who destroyed the pope when he urged that a holy war be waged against the Muslims? Was it not we who destroyed those madmen, the Knights Hospitallers, who believed that God wished them to wage war on the Muslims? Have we not been, throughout the ages, the friends of the Prophet (may God grant that his desires be fulfilled) and the enemy of his enemies? The

Mamelukes, for their part, have they not always rebelled against the authority of the Prophet, whom they continue, even now, to disown?'

Forty centuries are watching you...

Napoleon's speech showed him to be *au fait* with the situation in Egypt, which was currently under Mameluke rule.... The Mamelukes governed a nation of artisans, tradesmen and peasants chafing against a yoke that had become a mere anachronism. By the end of the 18th century Egypt's economic and political decadence was incontrovertible.

Conquering it, however, was not as easy as one might have anticipated. The preparations had been too hasty. The French invaded Egypt in July encumbered with equipment that was wholly inappropriate to the intense heat. Dysentery and a range of feverish conditions were rife among the troops, and all the evidence points to their being profoundly demoralized. We should not forget also that they had no real motivation for being in Egypt in the first place. This campaign was a far cry from Valmy or Jemmapes, where it had been a case of defending French native soil. It does nothing for an army's morale to know that it is expendable, and a number of the men took their own lives.

The victory at the Battle of the Pyramids, at the gates of Cairo, on 21 July, lifted flagging spirits. It was not until he was on St Helena, however, when he was dictating his memoirs, that Napoleon appears to have used the famous words 'Men ... forty centuries are watching you.' The enthusiasm was short-lived. On 1 August, the French fleet was attacked by Nelson in Aboukir Bay and almost entirely destroyed. The conqueror was now a prisoner of his conquest. This was real disaster. But

The entry of Napoleon into Cairo by G. Bourgouin, 1912.

Napoleon refused to be beaten. It was at this point that the most brilliant period of the entire expedition began. Under the direction of its commander-in-chief, a programme was initiated for developing Egypt.

After the Battle of the Pyramids, four military hospitals were set up at Giza and Bulaq and in Cairo and Old Cairo. The administration's books had to be balanced, and taxation was standardized and assessed according to the value of a piece of land. A population census was carried out and artisans and tradesmen, who had previously bought their 'protection' from the janissaries, were henceforth answerable exclusively to the military tribunals, and thereby protected from further extortions.

In order to continue subsidizing the costs of his army, Napoleon had no hesitation in seizing Mameluke property. The French took over the Customs House at Cairo. Gold bullion had been brought from France and exchanged in Alexandria for local currency. Napoleon now ordered General Kléber to buy back the gold with foodstuffs and to send it to Cairo, where a mint, under the direction of Monge, Berthollet and Costaz, would convert it into coins. The funds thus collected would be supplemented by emergency taxes levied against the different guilds.

Every effort was made, moreover, to gain the sympathy of the Egyptian people. A respect for their religious beliefs was one of the most salient characteristics of the French occupation. The feudal system established by the Mamelukes was swept aside, and in its place a major construction programme set up. The engineer Charles Lepère examined the possibility of linking the Red Sea and the Mediterranean across the Isthmus of Suez. Canals were recut to carry water to land under cultivation. On the intellectual front, Napoleon, who signed all his proclamations as a member of the Institut, founded an Egyptian Institute on the French model. Newspapers were also published....

But the focus was, above all, on Egypt's past.... The archaeological excavations at ancient Thebes, modern Luxor and Karnak, the discovery of the Rosetta Stone, and the drawings done by Vivant Denon's team for the *Description of Egypt*, all demonstrate the lively curiosity felt even by simple soldiers for that lost world.

How were all these activities possible, given the expedition's limited resources?

As the occupation spread, the position of Napoleon's troops became increasingly precarious. Jullien, the aide-de-camp sent to liaise with Kléber, was assassinated along with his escort in Menouf province. The French garrison at el Mansura was attacked and massacred, and the troops at Damietta narrowly escaped a similar fate. The Cairo uprising, on 21 October, cost General Dupuy and Napoleon's favourite aide-de-camp, Sulkowski, their lives.

In September 1798 rumours reached Cairo of heavy concentrations of Turkish troops in Syria. Napoleon decided on a pre-emptive strike. At the same time, by pushing on as far as Constantinople, he planned to assemble a fleet to take him back to France. He stormed the ports of Gaza and Jaffa and routed the Turkish army at Mount Tabor, near Nazareth, on 16 April 1799. But then came the stumbling block: St John of Acre, a fortress defended by the émigré Louis-Edmond Phélipeaux, which was receiving supplies from the English fleet under the command of Sir Sidney Smith. The driving force behind the resistance was

Ahmed Djezzar, the Pasha of Acre, Tripoli and Damascus. The French stormed the first rampart, but the enemy constructed a second defensive wall centred on the fortress of Djezzar itself. Napoleon's lack of artillery resources was a serious handicap, and after two months he was forced to abandon the siege, a decision that was no doubt reinforced by the imminent prospect of Turkish troops landing on Egyptian soil.

It was a badly demoralized army which retreated from St John of Acre, an army burdened with sick and wounded men. The plague was claiming numerous victims, as Napoleon made no attempt to conceal in his report to the Directoire of 28 June 1799: 'The plague began at Alexandria, six months ago, with very marked symptoms. At Damietta, its violence abated. At Gaza and Jaffa, it claimed more victims. There was no sign of it at Cairo or Suez or in Upper Egypt. In consequence, the French army, from the time of its arrival in Egypt until the 10th of *Messidor*, year VII [28 June 1799], has lost 5344 men. The Syrian campaign has been highly successful: we are masters of the entire desert, and we have frustrated the plans of our enemies for the duration of this year. But we have lost some distinguished men. General Bon died of his wounds; Caffarelli is dead; my aide-de-camp Croizier is dead; and many men have been wounded.' The object of this letter was to request reinforcements, an indication that Napoleon had not yet lost heart. In it he also gave an account of the links he had attempted to establish with Mecca, the Indies and Mauritius. But did he really have any illusions about the likelihood of the Directoire sending him reinforcements when it was once more in the grip of a war on the home front? There was no certainty even of the letter

Denon measuring the Great Sphinx, Giza. Right: Napoleon's cavalry at Karnak.

reaching Paris.

It was with such resources as he still had at his disposal that Napoleon succeeded in overwhelming the Turkish forces landing at Aboukir. This new victory blotted out the former defeat in that same bay, but his lack of troops meant that there could be no future for Napoleon in the East: militarily, it was a dead end. According to Miot, Napoleon summoned Murat the night before the conflict and declared: 'This battle will decide the fate of the world' — a remark whose significance Murat did not immediately grasp. Having received notice, on 17 August, that the enemy's ships were no longer cruising off Alexandria and Aboukir, Napoleon made up his mind.... [On] the 22nd [he] notified the army of his intentions: 'to [leave] the army under the command of General Kléber. I will keep the army informed of my activities....'

Jean Tulard
History, November 1983

The Description of Egypt

The 'Description of Egypt' was published by the imperial printing house on Napoleon's orders. It took 200 artists to prepare the 907 plates, comprising a total of more than 3000 illustrations. The aim of the book was to show Egypt from a whole range of different angles: monuments, plant and animal life, landscapes, work, everyday objects....

Three volumes of plates and two volumes of text are devoted to the natural history of Egypt. Theban eagle (left); doum palm (top); waterlily *Nymphaea nelumbo* (centre).

Frontispiece (right). A panoramic view, showing the principal monuments of Egypt, from Alexandria to the Cataract.

The members of Napoleon's expedition were clearly eager to understand the customs and working methods of contemporary Egyptians, since two volumes of plates and three volumes of text provide an overview of life in Egypt at the end of the 18th century. Far page: Methods of irrigation. This page, from top to bottom (left): Making pipe cleaners; grinding tobacco; basket making.

Unwinding wool and spinning (above).

The Egyptian Revival style

Or how a military campaign gave rise to a new decorative style.... Napoleon returned to Paris, and was elected consul. His triumph was now assured and the decorative arts were quick to mirror, and to crystallize, this triumph in an individual style that encompassed architecture, furnishings and ornaments. The basis for this new style was an Egyptomania pushed to its very limits.

Miniature replica of one of the pylons at Edfu, a cabinet to house gold coins (above). Ebony incrusted with silver. Chair designed in imitation of Egyptian mortuary furnishings (below).

Torch bearer in gilded wood reminiscent of the statues decorating the façades of Egyptian tombs.

Black bronze candelabrum in the shape of a kneeling Nubian woman. When this piece was produced, no one could read the faithfully rendered hieroglyphs on its base.

Grey and gold Sèvres inkstand decorated with funerary figures.

Gilded bronze inkstand with sphinxes that belonged to Talleyrand.

The obelisk's long journey

In October 1836 a new monument was erected at the centre of the Place de la Concorde in Paris, and notices were posted around the city inviting Parisians to attend the ceremony. The monument, a gift from the government of Egypt, was the Luxor obelisk. In 1878 the English followed suit, erecting the obelisk they had been given, Cleopatra's Needle, on the Thames Embankment, London.

The Luxor obelisk: material and dimensions

The obelisk is made of fine red granite, quarried at Aswan, in southern Egypt, at the First Cataract. It is a monolith, that is, cut from a single block of granite. The surface of each side is highly polished and slightly convex; the base is square and the shaft then tapers towards the top and ends in a small pyramidion.

Each of its four surfaces carries three columns of ancient Egyptian hieroglyphs. The hieroglyphs of the central column are quite deeply carved and are perfectly polished; those in the flanking columns are cut to a lesser depth. The total number of characters is 1600 and the inscriptions read from top to bottom.

The obelisk is 72 feet tall and weighs 254 tons. This impressive monument was constructed in *c.* 1550 BC, in the reign of Tuthmosis III, who has been called 'the Napoleon of ancient Egypt'.

The organization of the French ceremony

Once the obelisk has been raised to the correct height vis-à-vis its intended pedestal, it can be set in place in a matter of hours.

It will be a curious sight to which Parisians will now be treated: this massive block of stone being raised into the air as it responds, with mathematical precision, to the turning movement imparted to it. Imagine the lid of a snuff box opening bit by bit and, as it turns on its hinge, coming to rest at a right angle to the rest of the box. This, precisely, will be the movement described by the monolith. From a horizontal position, it will be levered against a piece of curved wood – a hinge of sorts – so that it rises little by little into the air, until finally achieving a state of perfect equilibrium in

The two obelisks at Luxor (opposite). The obelisk being taken down (above left). The beginning of its journey to the Nile, protected by a wooden frame (right).

relation to its base. Ten winches will be used, each one operated by thirty gunners, making three hundred men in all. M. Lebas [the engineer] will take up a position on the pedestal and direct operations himself using a megaphone. It is easy to see just how precise the movements will have to be and how punctual the men's response to his orders. No threats will be needed; patriotism combined with intelligence, even more than perfect discipline, will be a sufficiently powerful driving force for Lebas' orders to be executed down to the last detail.

The area between the obelisk and the railings of the Pont Tournant will be turned into a semicircular enclosure which can hold two thousand people. The remainder of the Place de la Concorde, Rue Royale, the Pont de la Révolution and the terraces of the Tuileries will be opened up to the public.

The obelisk will be erected on Saturday 22 October 1836.

Public notice, Paris, October 1836

Transporting Cleopatra's Needle

The design of a vessel is generally made to meet the requirements of the service on which she will be employed at sea. In this particular case, however, the builders had the novel experience of constructing a seaworthy craft in which every thing had to be subordinated to the one prime feature that would enable her to be launched by rolling down the beach. That is to say, the vessel had to be perfectly cylindrical; stability and other desirable qualities had to be obtained mostly by internal arrangements. Were the axis of the Needle to coincide with the axis of the cylinder, it is evident that when once started rolling in the water, it would keep on almost indefinitely, retarded and finally stopped only by the skin resistance. By bringing the centre of gravity of the Needle below that axis, the vessel would be in a state of stable equilibrium; that is to say, however much the wind and sea might careen it over, the action of gravity would bring it back to the vertical; and this would obtain until the vessel were actually upside down. The lower the weight, the greater the righting force, and therefore the greater stability, but also the more violent rolling motion....

In order to ease the pitching motion as much as possible, the bed of the obelisk

View of the *Louxor* being towed from Alexandria to Le Havre by the *Sphinx* (above). The obelisk being erected in the Place de la Concorde (opposite).

was also prepared so that it would lie with the thick end forward. The centre of gravity of the Needle being at about one third its height from the base, and being naturally placed in the centre of the vessel (in regard to its length), the upper or longer end would extend farther from that centre, or nearer to the end of the vessel, than would the larger and shorter end; therefore putting the latter forward would throw less weight into the bows than the small end would bring. The lines of the bow were also made as full as was consistent with a reasonable expenditure of power in towing....

Erecting Cleopatra's Needle

Work was commenced on the apparatus for erecting the Needle. First of all, four immense uprights were fashioned, each formed of six heavy balks of timber over sixty feet high and a foot square, strengthened and braced together by tie-beams, and supported in their vertical position by struts thrown out on all sides. These uprights were to do duty as guide-rods for the carriage, so to speak, on

which the obelisk would be borne aloft and held while turning This carriage consisted of two horizontal box-girders, one on either side of the stone, supported on wooden blocking fitted in between the balks composing the uprights. A wrought-iron jacket, twenty feet long, was riveted round the Needle, from which projected on opposite sides, at the centre of gravity, two knife-edge pivots, which should rest on the box-girders. The jacket was made twenty feet long, to guard against any possible danger of the Needle being fractured by the weight of its own ends. Wooden packing was driven in between it and the sides of the monolith to save the surface of the stone from injury. To prevent the middle from slipping through while being swung into a vertical position, a stirrup-strap was passed round the base from two sides of the jacket. The object in having the movable girders take the weight during the operation was to afford the means of lowering the Needle on the pedestal after being swung into the vertical. Hydraulic jacks under the girders would effect this easily. As soon as the scaffolding was ready the monolith was slowly raised in a horizontal position by hydraulic jacks, being followed up in the ascent by timber-blocking....When the obelisk reached such a height that on being turned the heel would be several inches above and clear of the pedestal, controlling tackles were secured to both heel and point, and, a preliminary trial on the 11th proving successful, September 12th was fixed upon for the erection. The time was three p.m. An inopportune shower coming on suddenly early in the afternoon somewhat thinned out the crowd that had begun to assemble; but the sun reappeared, and, under the pleasant auspices of a clearing sky, a vast concourse lined the river front. At the appointed hour the controlling tackles were handled, and in half an hour the obelisk was vertical. The Union Jack and Turkish flag were run up in token of success, and ringing cheers bespoke the congratulations of the multitude. The operation of lowering the monument to the pedestal was deferred until the following day, and was then performed with complete success.

H. H. Gorringe
Egyptian Obelisks, 1882

Cleopatra's Needle, Alexandria (above). Mohammed Ali offered it to the English in 1820, but it remained in Alexandria until the engineer John Dixon devised a means of transport.

The *Cleopatra* in trouble in the bay of Biscay (main picture). Built by Dixon in 1875, the 'ship', towed by the *SS Olga*, comprised a metal cylinder topped by a bridge, mast and sails. The 200-ton obelisk being raised on the Victoria Embankment beside the Thames, 12 September 1878

The inauguration of the Suez Canal

The creation of a direct link between the Mediterranean and the Red Sea was an idea dating back to the time of the pharaohs. This dream was finally realized by Ferdinand de Lesseps (below), a former French consul-general in Alexandria, in 1869. The ceremonies marking the opening of the 164km canal were reported by 'The Illustrated London News'.

The Imperial and Royal visitors to the Isthmus of Suez, hospitably entertained by the Khedive [Viceroy] as ruler of Egypt, and by M. Ferdinand de Lesseps, as Chairman of the Canal Company, were conducted, in a procession of steamships, from sea to sea....The Empress Eugénie, both as a lady of the most exalted rank and as the wife of Napoleon III, embarked on the French Imperial yacht, *Aigle*, which conveyed her [from Alexandria] to Port Said.... As the *Aigle* entered the port the salute began.... For an hour there was almost incessant cannonading....The religious ceremony of pronouncing a benediction upon the canal...took place at three o'clock the same afternoon....The illumination and display of fireworks at Port Said that evening was splendid....Wednesday morning, Nov. 17, the eventful day...broke bright and clear....The *Aigle*, with the French Empress on board, started punctually at eight o'clock, and was followed in regular order by the ships [bearing dignitaries and representing other countries]...all arrived safely at Ismailia, the midway port in Lake Timsah....Thursday morning showed the strange little town of Ismailia in festive attire. The Empress of the French, the Emperor of Austria, and the other great persons landed early from their ships, and were conducted by the Khedive to his new palace lately built for the occasion....The Viceroy entertained their Majesties and Royal Highnesses, at night, with a sumptuous ball.... attended by several thousand people.... Of the miscellaneous fleet of vessels collected at Ismailia, some moved on towards Suez the next day...which they reached at eleven o'clock on Saturday, the 20th....

The Illustrated London News
11 December 1869

The first convoy of ships (top) to sail along the Suez Canal was headed by the French *Aigle* carrying the Empress Eugénie. An engraving published at the time of the completion of the canal in 1869 (above) shows the three pavilions specially built at Port Said for the gala opening by the Empress Eugénie and the blessing of the canal by Muslim and Christian religious leaders.

...gers, travellers and ... of earlier years there arose an English giant, Sir William Matthew Flinders Petrie (1852-1942), whose researches and working methods were to lay the foundations of modern Egyptology.

Flinders Petrie's greatest contribution was to bring order into the chaos of Egyptological research. His was the first systematic archaeological work in the Near East and he spent over forty years excavating there, first in Egypt and subsequently in Palestine.

Petrie's output was prodigious and he is credited with more than a thousand books, articles and reviews. Though he had no formal education, he was to become, by the terms of the will of Amelia Edwards, the holder of the first Egyptological Chair in Britain, the Edwards Chair of Egyptology in University College London, from 1892 until 1933.

He paid incredible attention to detail, and was quite prepared to go back to excavate sites previously 'examined' simply to make a true and correct record. It was in the course of one such exercise, planning and reclearing the early dynastic tombs at Abydos ravaged by the Frenchman Amelineau, that he discovered royal jewelry of the Ist dynasty.

Peter A. Clayton

Sovereigns for a queen's bracelet

The most important discovery this year [made on 28 November 1900] is that of the jewellery in the tomb of King Zer [Djer] which belonged to his queen. While my workmen were clearing the tomb they noticed amongst the rubbish which they were moving a piece of the arm of a mummy in its wrappings. It lay in a broken hole in the north wall of the tomb.... The party of four who found it looked in to the end of the wrappings and saw a large gold bead, the rosette in the second bracelet. They did not yield to the natural wish to search further or to remove it; but laid the arm down where

Flinders Petrie (above) excavating in the Ramesseum at Thebes in December 1895. This tiny statuette (opposite), the only known portrait of Cheops, was found by Petrie at Abydos.

they found it until Mr. Mace should come and verify it. Nothing but obtaining the complete confidence of the workmen, and paying them for all they find, could ever make them deal with valuables in this careful manner. On seeing it Mr. Mace told them to bring it to our huts intact, and I received it quite undisturbed. In the evening the most intelligent of the party was summoned up as a witness of the opening of the wrappings, so that there should be no suspicion that I had not dealt fairly with the men. I then cut open the bandages, and found, to our great surprise, the four bracelets of gold and jewellery, in the order in which they are shown upon the arm. The verification of the exact order of threading occupied an hour or two, working with a magnifier, my wife and

Mr. Mace assisting. When recorded, the gold was put in the scales and weighed against sovereigns before the workmen who saw everything. Rather more than the value of gold was given to the men, and thus we ensured their goodwill and honesty for the future. The sequel is instructive. Though all our camp of workers knew about this and about several other finds of gold, yet the willing separation between our workmen (who came from Koptos fifty miles away) and the local natives was so complete that no tales of the gold got about the country. When the Arabic papers copied the discovery from my letter in *The Times*, after I had left Egypt, it caused a great ferment in the neighbourhood and huge tales of the gold and treasures rent the hearts of the local plunderers, who till then were in ignorance of the valuables that my men had found. There can be no more satisfactory hold over the workmen than that which is proved by this whole affair.

W. M. F. Petrie
The Royal Tombs of the Earliest Dynasties
pt 2, 1901

Petrie recounted the Cairo Museum sequel in his autobiography 'Seventy Years in Archaeology' of 1931.

When Quibell came over on behalf of the Museum, I sent up the bracelets by him. The arm – the oldest mummified piece known – and its marvellously fine tissue of linen was also delivered to the Museum. Brugsch [assistant conservator in the Cairo Museum] only cared for display; so from one bracelet he cut away the half that was of plaited gold wire, and he also threw away the arm and the linen. A museum is a dangerous place [!].

The Princess's mud-encased jewelry and a problem of division

In earlier years any excavated finds of major importance, artistic or historical significance naturally went to the Cairo Museum. The authorities would then divide any remaining items between Cairo and the excavating body. In this way Petrie and others were able to attract funds for excavation by allocating objects allowed them to their sponsors. Invariably the Egyptian authorities were extremely generous in the objects they allowed to leave Egypt.

On February 10 a tomb was being cleared [on the south side of the pyramid of Senusret II] which had been plundered anciently; the sarcophagus was empty, and nothing was anticipated. In clearing a recess (of about a cubic yard)

at the side, which was filled with hard mud washed down into the tomb, a few rings of thin gold tubing were found, and at once reported. I turned out the local workers, and only left a Qufti lad. As, owing to a strain, I could not go down, [Guy] Brunton went to see what the meaning of the place might be. He continued carefully to cut away the mud and found more gold work, and slept all night in the tomb. I said the Qufti was not to go to camp till I saw him. Near midnight he came up, and I promised him 30 in any case, and much more if he said nothing. That secured his silence, so that even his own brother could not find out what he had.

For a week Brunton lived all day and every night in the tomb, gently extracting all the objects from the hard mud, without bending or scratching a single piece. Everything as it came up I washed in plain water with a camel-hair brush, so as not to alter the natural surface, and then photographed it. I packed the whole in a tin box by the 17th, and next day Campion took up the sealed box to the safe of the [Cairo] Museum. Our party were all warned not to talk or write about it, and there was no stir anywhere on the subject.

When we came to the division in Cairo, [Sir Gaston] Maspero [Director of the Cairo Museum] was startled and said: 'Why, you have got the Dahshur jewellery over again.' We agreed on division, the Museum leaving to us all duplicates of the gold work, but the halving left us with the silver mirror with obsidian and gold handle; Maspero coveted it, so I offered to resign that against the commoner things we had found. No one but my wife knows how we transferred the jewellery to London.

The only persons whom I informed of the find were the directors of three

Petrie returns to Abydos, aged 69, in 1922.

Museums, which had shared in our work before. Obviously the set liberated at Cairo should be kept together; but there were many Museums who were creditors to the work. The only course was for one Museum to indemnify the others by payment to us, so that the other Museums should receive compensation in other antiquities that we then, and in the future, could provide. Of the three Museums, I named in writing to the British Museum 8,000 as the least value of what we had found, but no such amount to the other two Museums.

In a few weeks, exactly that valuation had been conveyed to the dealers in Luqsor, a direct incitement to attack us by the many predatory parties who fought the guards at different places for objects of only a hundredth of that value. How the information was conveyed one may guess....

Then came the smash of all civil matters by the War. We waited to see what could best be done; the Committee left negotiations to me, with a condition that any English Museum was to have a preference of 2,000 over any foreign Museum....Having waited for a couple of years without any response in England, we reluctantly accepted an offer from the Metropolitan Museum of New York, which was one of our contributing Museums.... The apathy of all authorities in England and the futile replies received from the British Museum and South Kensington [Victoria and Albert Museum] left no better course open than that which we took. The great importance of the finest treasure of Egyptian jewellery known makes a clear account of the matter necessary.

W.M.F. Petrie
Seventy Years in Archaeology, 1931

The American assault on the pyramids

On 8 June 1867 a young American journalist, Samuel Langhorne Clemens (below), who was just beginning to make a name for himself under the pseudonym Mark Twain, set sail on the 'Quaker City' for the first organized grand tour in the history of tourism.

A laborious walk in the flaming sun brought us to the foot of the great Pyramid of Cheops. It was a fairy vision no longer. It was a corrugated, unsightly mountain of stone. Each of its monstrous sides was a wide stairway which rose upward, step above step, narrowing as it went, till it tapered to a point far aloft in the air. Insect men and women – pilgrims from the *Quaker City* – were creeping about its dizzy perches, and one little black swarm were waving postage stamps from the airy summit – handkerchiefs will be understood.

Of course we were besieged by a rabble of muscular Egyptians and Arabs who wanted the contract of dragging us to the top – all tourists are. Of course you could not hear your own voice for the din that was around you. Of course the Sheiks said *they* were the only responsible parties; that all contracts must be made with them, all moneys paid over to them, and none exacted from us by any but themselves alone. Of course they contracted that the varlets who dragged us up should not mention bucksheesh once. For such is the usual routine. Of course we contracted with them, paid them, were delivered into the hands of the draggers, dragged up the Pyramids, and harried and be-deviled for bucksheesh from the foundation clear to the summit. We paid it, too, for we were purposely spread very far apart over the vast side of the Pyramid. There was no help near if we called, and the Herculeses who dragged us had a way of asking sweetly and flatteringly for bucksheesh, which was seductive, and of looking fierce and threatening to throw us down the precipice, which was persuasive and convincing. Each step being full as high as a dinner-table; there being very, very many of the steps; an Arab having hold of each of our arms and springing upward from step to step and snatching us with them, forcing us to lift our feet as high as our breasts every time, and do it rapidly and keep it up till we were ready to faint, who shall say it is not lively, exhilarating, lacerating, muscle-straining, bone-wrenching and perfectly excruciating and exhausting pastime, climbing the Pyramids? I beseeched the varlets not to twist *all* my joints asunder; I iterated, reiterated, even *swore* to them that I did not wish to beat any body to the top; did all I could to convince them that if I got there the last of all I would feel blessed above men and grateful to them forever; I begged them, prayed them, pleaded with them to let me stop and rest a moment – only one little moment: and they only answered with some more frightful springs....Twice, for one minute, they let me rest while they extorted bucksheesh, and then continued their maniac flight up the Pyramid. They wished to beat the other parties. It was nothing to them that I, a stranger, must be sacrificed upon the altar of their unholy ambition. But in the midst of sorrow, joy blooms. Even in this dark hour I had a sweet consolation. For I knew that except these Mohammedans repented they would go straight to perdition some day. And *they* never repent – they never forsake their paganism. This thought calmed me, cheered me, and I sank down, limp and exhausted, upon the summit, but happy, *so* happy and serene within.

Mark Twain, *The Innocents Abroad*, 1875

A tourist climbing the pyramid of Cheops in *c.* 1900. With each block measuring between 65 cm and 90 cm in depth (while the average step measures 20 cm), climbing them was no easy task! The tourists seem to have been undaunted, however, and in 1870 the American consulate in Cairo registered the arrival of three hundred American visitors.

The greatest excavator of his day

Just five months after Mark Twain climbed the Great Pyramid, an American Egyptologist was born in Indianapolis who would reveal the secrets of the Giza pyramid field.

George Andrew Reisner, born 5 November 1867, was to be hailed as the greatest American Egyptological excavator ever. His attention to detail meant that his reports and publications necessarily took longer to complete and, at his death on 6 June 1942 at his beloved Giza, he left numerous publications unfinished.

Reisner's greatest works concerned pyramids. Amongst his discoveries in Lower Nubia were the pyramids of no fewer than sixty-eight Ethiopian kings, but it is with Giza that he will be for ever associated. Here he excavated the Valley Temple of Mykerinus, builder of the third pyramid, where he found remarkable statuary of the pharaoh. Perhaps his greatest triumph, on 2 February 1925, was the discovery of the tomb of Queen Hetep-heres, mother of Khufu (Cheops), the builder of the Great Pyramid.

The discovery, in its way as exciting as that of Tutankhamun's tomb, came about by accident. The expedition's photographer was endeavouring to find a firm footing for his tripod to the east of the Great Pyramid when he realized that one of the three feet was finding a better purchase than the other two: it was sinking into plaster rather than scraping on natural rock!

The reconstructed carrying chair of Queen Hetep-heres, found in her tomb at Giza and now in the Cairo Museum. Reisner discovered magnificent gilded tomb furniture at the bottom of a deep shaft in 1925.

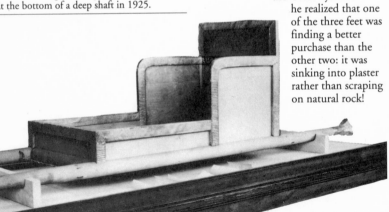

Investigation revealed the concealed opening to a 27 metre-shaft with a small tomb chamber, only 5.22 x 2.70 metres, opening off at the bottom of it.

The excavators' first view of the chamber was one of confusion: along the left-hand wall stood a large alabaster sarcophagus with, beyond it, a square canopic chest that had held the Queen's internal organs removed during her embalming (actually the earliest evidence we have of evisceration being practised). On top of the sarcophagus was a series of gold-encased poles and, to the side, closely packed, were fragments of furniture similarly inlaid with gold and numerous pottery and alabaster vessels. Reisner's meticulous approach and detailed recording of the remains in the chamber meant that it was not until two years after the discovery, on 3 March 1927, that a small group of eight people could crowd into the tiny chamber for the opening of the alabaster sarcophagus. Slowly the heavy flat lid was raised and the audience peered eagerly into the deep interior of the box – only to find it empty, and no sign of the body of the great queen.

Peter A. Clayton

Why then this chamber crowded with her funerary furniture? Why then the deep concealed pit? Why then the crowding of mortuary objects into so constrained a space? When Khufu had this secret tomb prepared beside his pyramid had he known that his mother's sarcophagus was empty? We shall never know the answers to these questions, but Reisner composed an ingenious theory to embrace all the facts. The husband of Queen Hetep-heres, King Snefru, had been buried at Dahshur fifteen miles south of Gizeh. It is reasonable that she herself was first laid away beside her husband at Dahshur. Then her son Khufu transferred his attention to his own burial place, the Gizeh Plateau. Dahshur was abandoned under the protection of the funerary priests and cemetery guards. Perhaps then human greed entered; the responsible guards and priests obligingly looked the other way, and robbers violated the Queen's tomb. They seized upon the mummy, carried it out somewhere into the desert, and stripped it of the jewelry and ornaments on the body. Then some one not in on the conspiracy hastily reassembled the things in the tomb, put the lid back on the sarcophagus, and reported to the King. In terror of his life, this informant dared not say that the Queen's body had disappeared. He perhaps reported that robbers had attempted an entry, had been caught in the act and killed. He recommended that Hetep-heres be reburied in a place of greater safety.

Following the theory, Khufu accepted the statement that his mother still lay in her sarcophagus and ordered a secret and hasty reburial beside himself at Gizeh. No one, up to the Vizier himself, dared risk his life by telling the King that her body was missing. In all solemn secrecy, the sarcophagus, the funerary equipment, the carrying chair, the two armchairs, the bed and its canopy, the various boxes, jars, and tools were brought from Dahshur and reburied in the little chamber at Gizeh, to rest for forty-five hundred years. It is a theory of beautiful reasoning, which, alas, cannot be tested as a modern detective might follow up his reasoning.

John A. Wilson
Signs and Wonders upon Pharaoh, 1964

The Serapeum at Memphis

One day, noticing the heads of some sphinxes sticking out of the sand at Saqqara, Auguste Mariette (below) remembered a reference by Strabo to the tomb of the Apis Bulls at Memphis. He decided to start excavating. In November 1851, after having actually located the site of the avenue and cleared it of sand, he found a series of huge underground galleries.

A visit to Memphis in 30 BC

Memphis...contains temples, one of which is that of Apis, who is the same as Osiris; it is here that the bull Apis is kept in a kind of sanctuary, being regarded, as I have said, as god; his forehead and certain other small parts of his body are marked with white, but the other parts are black; and it is by these marks that they always choose the bull suitable for the succession, when the one that holds the honour has died. In front of the sanctuary is situated a court, in which there is another sanctuary belonging to the bull's mother. Into this court they set Apis loose at a certain hour, particularly that he may be shown to foreigners; for although people can see him through the window in the sanctuary, they wish to see him outside also; but when he has finished a short bout of skipping in the court they take him back again to his familiar stall.

There is here, then, not only the temple of Apis, which lies near the Hephaesteium, but also the Hephaesteium itself, which is a costly structure both in the size of its naos and in all other respects. In front, in the dromus, stands also a colossus made of one stone; and it is the custom to hold bull-fights in this dromus, and certain men breed these bulls for the purpose, like horse-breeders; for the bulls are set loose and join in combat, and the one that is regarded as victor gets a prize.

Strabo, XVII, 31

Looking down from the citadel at Cairo, Mariette took the decision to begin excavating

It was extraordinarily peaceful. The city stretched away before me. A heavy mist seemed to have fallen, shrouding all the houses, even the rooftops.

Out of this deep ocean rose three hundred minarets like the masts of a submerged fleet. Far to the south the date groves could be seen, their roots tangling with the ruins of Memphis. To the west, hazed in the fiery and golden light of the setting sun, stood the pyramids. It was an imposing sight. I was so struck by it, so utterly absorbed, that the violence of the experience was almost painful. I hope I may be forgiven for indulging in details that are perhaps too personal; if I dwell on them, it is because this moment was a real turning point. Before me lay Giza, Abusir, Saqqara, Dahshur and Mit-Rahineh. The dream of a whole lifetime was taking shape. There, almost within reach of my hand, lay a whole world of tombs, of stelae, inscriptions, statues. What more can I say?

The next day, I had hired two or three mules for the baggage, and a couple of donkeys for myself; I had bought a tent, a few cases of provisions, all the impedimenta of a desert journey; and, during the day of 20 October 1850, I had my camp pitched at the foot of the Great Pyramid.

Auguste Mariette
The Serapeum at Memphis, 1856

He published an account, written for the public, of the project's development

View 1 was drawn during the excavations. The sand, piled up over the centuries, had hardened to such a degree that the walls of our trenches were very nearly vertical. Digging these trenches was not always a straightforward operation, however, and sometimes great lumps of sand would shear away and slide to the bottom, causing accidents. It will give the reader some idea of the interminable hold-ups that the

workmen's inexperience, our lack of tools and the nature of the sand caused us when he learns that in this section of the cutting opened along the avenue of sphinxes we advanced by less than a metre a week.

View 2 was taken from the main pylon of the Egyptian Serapeum, looking east. Prior to the start of excavations, everything that can be seen here was submerged in a layer of sand, the whole area forming a vast, featureless, sandy plain. The two escarpments to the right and left of the drawing show the original level of the sand that was piled on top of the structures. A wall on the right, still undiscovered at the time of this drawing, supported a whole series of strange symbolical animals.... It was at the eastern end of the supporting wall that the semicircle containing the statues of eleven Greek poets and philosophers was located. We should just note here that only in a temple to Serapis would it be

possible to find a chapel in the pure Greek style alongside a chapel in the pure Egyptian style. The bull removed from the naos, the splendid statue of Apis, is housed today in the Louvre. In front of the two chapels, the traces of a paved area can be seen. This was made up of long flat stones that had been fitted together with a certain amount of care. In May 1851, when we lifted up one of these stones, we saw that the sand beneath the paving was crammed full of bronze statuettes representing the gods of the Egyptian pantheon. In a single day, we collected 534 of them. The other parts of the temple were found to be similarly equipped. Since the Egyptians regarded sand as an impure substance, in all probability they were purifying the sand by placing images of their gods in it.

Illustration 3 shows the main gallery of the Apis tomb. This tomb, which is cut entirely out of the living rock, is made up in fact of several intersecting galleries. The majority of them form side chambers branching off to right and left, in which the divine mummies were deposited. The search for the Apis tomb was, almost from the outset, the constant focus of our preoccupations. The upheavals to which the Serapeum had

been subject, traces of which I had readily discerned, left little hope regarding the temple proper; the Apis tomb, on the other hand, hewn out of the rock as it was, ought to be more nearly preserved in its original condition. My hopes on this score were not disappointed. The Apis tomb was an entirely subterranean structure, and when, on 12 November 1851, I first entered it, I confess to experiencing a feeling of amazement from which even now, five years later, I have not wholly recovered. By some strange chance that I have difficulty explaining, a chamber in the tomb, walled up in the 30th year of Ramesses II, had escaped the looting to which the rest of the monument had fallen prey, and I had the good fortune to find it still intact. Three thousand seven hundred years had done nothing to change the original aspect of the place. The cement still bore the fingerprints of the Egyptian who had slotted in the final stone when the doorway was walled up. Bare feet had left their imprint on the layer of sand deposited in a corner of the mortuary chamber. For almost forty centuries now, an embalmed bull had reposed here, and in this its final resting place everything was intact. Many a

Illustrations taken from Mariette's *The Serapeum at Memphis* showing the tomb of the Apis Bulls: 1 – the site during excavations; 2 – the main pylon looking east; 3 – the main gallery; 4 – a side chamber.

Mariette was the first director of Cairo's earliest archaeological museum, at Bulaq (above). Archaeologists and foreign governments began to donate the fruits of their excavations to the museum. Mariette lived there, and was buried in the garden.

traveller would no doubt be intimidated by the prospect of living alone in a desert for four years. But discoveries like that of the chamber of Ramesses II evoke the sort of emotions beside which everything else pales into insignificance, the sort of emotions one longs to feel again and again. This tomb was worthy of the prince [Khaemwese, a son of Ramesses II] upon whose orders it was fitted out, and when one sees in the Louvre the magnificent jewels, the statuettes and vases we recovered from it, it is easy to grasp how later, when the cult of Serapis was at its height, it was possible, as Diodorus claims, to spend a sum of 500,000 francs [100 talents, approximately £25,000] on the funeral rites alone of an Apis bull.

Illustration 4 shows one of the side chambers of the Apis tomb. In the centre stands one of those enormous sarcophagi that are to be found throughout the tomb, and which date from the time of Amasis onwards. All are made of highly polished granite; they are twelve to thirteen feet tall, and fifteen to eighteen feet long, and the smallest weighs no less than sixty-five thousand kilograms [65 tonnes]. As regards the chambers themselves, there are sixty-four of them in all. The stones piled to form a wall over the top of the monument date, I believe, from the time of the tomb's looting. Following a custom still in force today in certain parts of the East, they were placed there as a sign of contempt after the corpse housed inside the monolith had been stripped of its belongings and then torn to pieces.

Auguste Mariette
The Serapeum at Memphis, 1856

The resurrection of Karnak

The vast citadel of the god Amun was likewise neglected and forgotten, its secrets veiled behind tumbling masonry and desert sand. Over the last four hundred years archaeologists have been uncovering those secrets little by little, bringing to light Karnak's original structures and piecing together what was once its great temple. Two of the archaeologists recently involved in the Karnak excavations retrace here the history of the site.

Visitors and excavators

Karnak. Summer 1589. A fierce sun was beating down as a man picked his way across to the great Hypostyle Hall. 'And as soon as I stepped inside and saw all those columns, I thought I must be dreaming! They were so thick! And all shaped like trees,' he wrote. His enthusiasm is not hard to understand. This man, a Venetian (we do not know his name), had just sailed up the Nile – facing innumerable dangers on the way – in order to see all those 'magnificent constructions' of which he had heard speak in Cairo. He was the first European to leave a record of his journey through Upper Egypt. Unfortunately, this travel account was not published or widely known. It remained hidden away in the archives and libraries of Italy until 1929, and future visitors to the region had no idea that they were following in the footsteps of a contemporary of Queen Elizabeth.

For almost a century no European travellers ventured into Upper Egypt, contenting themselves instead with visiting Lower Egypt and the ruins around Cairo, such as Giza and Saqqara. It was only by chance, during a tour of the various Coptic communities in Upper Egypt, that in 1668 two Capuchin friars, Fathers Francis and Protasius, discovered the ruins of Karnak

and Luxor. On his return to Cairo Father Protasius wrote an enthusiastic description of the ruins, which was published in 1672....

17th- and 18th-century scholars and sightseers

Karnak attracted a number of potential visitors from this date. The distance between Cairo and Luxor was considerable, however, and for foreigners the journey was fraught with dangers. In 1673 Father Vansleb, a German Dominican in the service of Louis XIV, was entrusted by Colbert with the task of collecting ancient manuscripts for the royal library; but, ignoring his mission, he left Cairo in an attempt to reach Luxor. Vansleb met with widespread hostility – the local population taking him for a dangerous magician – and was forced to retrace his steps. Others were luckier. Thus the Frenchman Paul Lucas, who combined the role of fortune hunter with those of pirate, Don Juan, trader, goldsmith, doctor and occasional explorer, succeeded in reaching Luxor in 1699 and again in 1717. But his description of Karnak is so confused that it casts some doubt on whether he actually visited the site....

We have to wait until 1722 for the arrival of a person capable of studying and identifying the ruins of Upper Egypt (though undoubtedly a less colourful character than 'Monsieur Paul'). The Jesuit scholar Claude Sicard possessed a detailed knowledge of the country and of its language and it is Sicard who can claim the credit for identifying the ruins of Luxor as the remains of ancient Thebes.

The number of travellers increased in the 18th century. The most remarkable journeys of the time were those undertaken by the Danish naval engineer Frederik Norden and the Anglican priest Richard Pococke, who were responsible for producing the first plans and drawings of Karnak. Europe had become obsessed with the East, and Thebes attracted numerous visitors right up until the end of the century. In 1759 an Italian doctor by the name of Donati excavated at Karnak on behalf of various Italian princes.

We owe the first truly scientific research and records, however, to the scholars who accompanied Napoleon to Egypt. In 1799 two young engineers, Jollois and Devilliers, devoted a great deal of their time to studying Karnak, a vast palace, as they and their companions saw it, where a wise and powerful sovereign had once dwelt. And the European public discovered the wonders of Karnak through the *Description of Egypt*'s magnificent illustrations – engravings which, though almost two centuries old, are still used by Egyptologists today.

Karnak in the 19th century

The history of 19th-century Karnak can be divided into three phases. Up until 1828 the site was looted by 'antiquaries' and traders taking advantage of the relative peace brought by Mohammed Ali's accession to power. The consuls of England (Henry Salt) and France (Bernardino Drovetti) engaged in a fierce struggle for possession of this promising excavation area, Salt hiring an Italian from Padua, the famous Giovanni Belzoni, to work for him. Belzoni's excavations made him enemies....

In 1828 Jean-Francois Champollion visited Karnak. By copying the texts that cover the walls of Amun's palace, bit by bit he brought its past to life; and the names of Karnak's builders – forgotten for twenty centuries – regained their

place in history. From 1828 to 1858, while the looting continued, travellers with more 'personal' motives were now joined by the first Egyptologists. Scientific missions came to study the temples, the most famous being that led by the German Karl Richard Lepsius in 1843. The same year as Lepsius' expedition, Prisse d'Avennes, part artist, part archaeologist, and part fortune hunter, dismantled the Table of the Kings at Karnak; in his eagerness to serve the 'interests of France', he had it taken back to Paris. Daguerreotypists and, from 1850, photographers made the pilgrimage to Upper Egypt, returning home with valuable documents. But the situation remained catastrophic. In 1840 the pylons of the southern avenue were still being used as a quarry.

Finally, in 1858, Auguste Mariette succeeded in halting the disaster. Having gained the trust of the viceroy Saïd, he was appointed Director of the Egyptian Antiquities Service, which was created at his behest. That same year, he began a series of major excavations in the heart of the temple of Amun. From now on, the excavations were planned so that one project would follow another in a systematic fashion (in 1860 excavations began on the great courtyard, Hypostyle Hall and central zone; in 1874, on the temple of Khonsu). Such efforts alone were not enough, however. Mariette's primary aim was to uncover historical documents; but the monuments also needed restoring. In 1861 a column in the recently excavated Hypostyle Hall had already collapsed. In 1865 it was a doorway situated between the 4th and 5th Pylons which caved in. There was an enormous amount of work to be done.

In 1895 Jacques de Morgan, one of Mariette's successors, set up a special body with responsibility for the site, the Direction des Travaux de Karnak. A young French Egyptologist, Georges Legrain, was put in charge.

Georges Legrain and his successors

Legrain bravely began a systematic excavation of the temple of Amun, from west to east, subjecting each monument to a thorough restoration as soon as it had been cleared of soil and rubble. Meanwhile, he kept an eye on the movements of the ground water from the river Nile. Nevertheless, on 3 October 1899, disaster struck: eleven columns in the Hypostyle Hall collapsed. Refusing to be beaten, Legrain devoted almost ten years of his life to repairing the damage and to strengthening the foundations of the Hypostyle Hall. Using extremely limited resources, and techniques – such as the construction of enormous earth mounds – that would not have been unfamiliar to his distant predecessors, Legrain succeeded in raising the collapsed columns in the Hypostyle Hall. The year 1903 was an auspicious one in the annals of Karnak. Buried in the courtyard before the 7th Pylon, Legrain discovered hundreds of statues of pharaohs and of Karnak's priests and officials dating from the different periods in its history [the Karnak cachette]. They had been buried at the beginning of the Ptolemaic era when they began to encumber the temple halls and courtyards. Switching between his roles of site manager, draughtsman, epigrapher, Egyptologist, technician, architect and even ethnologist, Legrain continued with the task of restoring Karnak right up to his death in 1917.

From 1921 to 1925 a French architect by the name of Maurice Pillet took over where Legrain had left off. The 3rd Pylon incorporated numerous older structures and thus provided a wealth of documentary evidence. In 1924 Pillet

narrowly avoided a fresh catastrophe in the southern half of the Hypostyle Hall. His successor, the architect H. Chevrier, director of the Travaux de Karnak from 1926 to 1954, had the great good fortune to discover, carefully dismantled and reincorporated in the 3rd Pylon, an absolute gem of Egyptian architecture: the wayside station or chapel of Sesostris I [1971-1928 BC]. Chevrier had the chapel re-erected in the open-air museum. Another happy chance led him to discover the extraordinary colossal statues of Amenophis IV [Akhenaten, 1379-1362 BC], to the east of the temple of Amun.

It would be a long and laborious job to list all the excavations that have taken place at Karnak in the course of the 20th century. To those of the Antiquities Service, then of the Egyptian Antiquities Organization...should be added the various foreign missions.... Despite appearances, however, all these missions have scarcely even scratched the surface of the site. The principal monuments have been excavated, but of the 123 hectares of the archaeological zone, only 14 hectares have been excavated down to the ancient soil level (11.4%). The deep excavations represent no more than 3.6 hectares, that is 2.9% of the total area excavated.

So, there may well be further surprises in store. Safeguarding Karnak, with all its architectural splendours, and continuing the work begun by Legrain must remain a major archaeological priority.

C. Traunecker and J.-C. Golvin
History and Archaeology, March 1982

The rebirth of Philae

When the island of Philae became a victim of 20th-century engineering works on the Nile, it no longer resembled the idyllic site described by travellers in former times. In 1960 UNESCO launched a successful campaign to save the site by transporting its monuments to the higher ground of a nearby island.

Before work began in 1972, the island of Philae was flooded all year round, the water level reaching a third of the way up its monuments. An enormous coffer dam, comprising two rows of steel plates, was built around the island, and between the steel plates a million cubic metres of sand were tipped; any water that seeped in was removed by pumping. Prior to being dismantled in some 40,000 sections, then transported to the nearby island of Agilkia, the monuments were cleaned and measured by photogrammetry, a special technique enabling the engineers to reconstruct their original appearance to within a millimetre of their actual size. The dismantling, transportation and reconstruction of the monuments (whose total weight was 27,000 tons, some of the blocks weighing up to 25 tons each) was carried out in a record two and a half years.

The monuments on Philae had remained intact since antiquity, but when the first dam was built on the Nile in 1898 and heightened in 1912, they were partially submerged. The situation worsened with each successive inundation and from 1934 to 1964 the Philae monuments stood half under water.

The rescue of Abu Simbel

The Egyptian government's decision to build a new dam at Aswan in 1956 threatened to destroy all the ancient sites and monuments along the Nubian stretch of the Nile.

Disaster was imminent, and, on 8 March 1960, UNESCO launched an international campaign to rescue Nubia's ancient sites and monuments. Thanks to the growing numbers of experienced Egyptologists worldwide, the member states of UNESCO were able to respond swiftly and positively to the appeal.

The dam was scheduled to be built in eight years' time; in the interim forty archaeological missions explored the threatened area and more than twenty monuments were saved, with the result that the archaeology of this part of Nubia is now the best known in the entire Nile valley.

Undoubtedly the most spectacular project in UNESCO's campaign involved the dismantling of the two rock-cut temples at Abu Simbel and the reconstruction of the temples and site on the plateau overlooking the new lake.

Moving the two temples was to prove an impressive feat of engineering

It has been observed that 'You can dismantle a temple, but you cannot dismantle a mountain.' The Abu Simbel temples were cut out of the sandstone cliff. The four seated colossi before the entrance to the Great Temple were hewn out of the solid rock, and the temple's inner chambers and chapels extended back more for than 60 m into the mountainside. Although smaller, the Temple of Queen Nefertari was fronted with six rock-cut colossi 10 m tall – the

The term 'colossus' is a particularly apt one for describing the statues of Abu Simbel. By comparing the relative size of the workmen and this section of Ramesses II's head (left), or the lower legs and feet of the statues fronting the Great Temple (right), we get an idea of the extraordinary dimensions of these figures. Individual sections weighed up to 20 tons.

A drawing showing the general plan of the site, and a photograph of the temples (the Great Temple on the left, the Small Temple on the right) in their new position, protected from potential flooding by a massive dyke. Two great concrete domes covered with rocks and sand were used to reconstruct the shape of the mountain out of which the temples had been cut.

height of a modern three-storey building! Those of the Great Temple are 20 m tall; their heads measure almost 4.2 m from ear to ear, and a person could sit quite comfortably inside one of these ears, which are more than a metre high! We might also note that each of the statues' eyes measures 84 cm, their noses 98 cm and their hands (resting flat on the knee) 2.64 m. Yet, despite their massive dimensions, these statues still have a natural grace. How were they to be moved?

Three different schemes were studied. The first involved leaving the temples where they were but building a huge transparent dome over them, so that they stood in the midst of an immense basin some 100 m deep. This counter-dam or dome, alone, would have cost as much as the new Aswan Dam. The second idea was to enclose the two temples in concrete caissons and cut the mountain away around and beneath the gigantic block thus created; this would then be raised by jacks and, like some monstrous cake, transported to its ultimate resting place on the plateau. The third, and

marginally less laborious, approach was the one finally selected. The aim here was to detach all the sculpted and decorated temple sections by cutting them away from the mountain. The blocks – none of which would weigh more than twenty tons – would be transported to their new site by means of cranes and trucks. A landscape as similar as possible to the original one would then be created around them. The Abu Simbel temples, removed and transported like pieces of a giant jigsaw puzzle, now stand approximately 200 m from their original site, and to facilitate access to them an airport, complete with a small hotel, has been built close by.

The first sight of Abu Simbel, 1813

It was the Swiss traveller Johann Ludwig Burckhardt who, in 1813, while in Nubia disguised as a Syrian merchant by the name of Ibrahim Ibn Abdallah, first saw and described the site of Abu Simbel, or Ipsambal as he called it.

Greek mercenaries in the Egyptian army had admired Abu Simbel and carved their names on the legs of one of

Temple of Abu Simbel (above) and Queen Nefertari's temple (right).

the southern colossi in 591 BC, during a military campaign waged by Psammeticus II against the Sudanese pharaoh Aspelta. The temple was already beginning to disappear behind drifts of sand at this date. Henceforth, the very existence of Abu Simbel seems to have faded from men's memories. None of the classical authors, Greek or Roman, speaks of it. In 1799 the Nubian Haggi Mohammed, when questioned by the scholars on the French expedition, drew up a long list of Nubian villages between the First and the Second Cataract; he cites 'Absimbil', but mentions no ruins, while specifying their existence at numerous other sites, such as Kertassi, Debod, Taffa, Kalabsha, Derr and Kasr Ibrim, whose temples are of much less importance than those of Abu Simbel.

When, following the instructions given him by local Arabs, Burckhardt finally reached Abu Simbel on 22 March 1813, he approached it by the high desert plateau and, making his way down into the valley, visited the Small Temple, that of Queen Nefertari, which was the only one he had heard mentioned. He described this shrine at length in his journal, and then added: 'Having, as I imagined, seen all Ipsambal's antiquities, I was preparing to return by the same

path that I had taken on my way down when, by great good fortune, taking a slight detour to the south, I came across what remains visible of four vast colossal statues hewn out of the mountainside some 200 m from the temple [of Nefertari]. They stand in a deep cutting in the mountainside. It is a great pity that they are now almost entirely covered in sand. An entire head and part of the breast and arms of one of the statues emerge still above the surface. Of the adjacent statue, there is almost nothing to be seen, since its head has broken off and its body is covered in sand to above shoulder level. Of the two others, only their headdresses are visible. It is difficult to decide whether these statues are seated or standing.'

Thus, in 1813, the Nubians themselves no longer knew about the Great Temple, and the latter was buried so deep in sand that Burckhardt was not even sure whether it actually existed. In his own words, 'Against the rock wall, in the midst of the four colossi, is the statue of Osiris, with his falcon head surmounted by a disc, and, beneath this statue, if we could move away the sand, I suspect that we might find a huge temple, with the four colossal statues probably serving to decorate the entrance.'

It seemed that no one would ever be able to shift the huge quantity of sand masking the temple's façade

Millions of cubic metres of sand had

piled up against the mountainside and the temple, and, in 1813, no mechanical means were available for removing it. It would have required hundreds of men to shift it and Nubia, which was virtually uninhabited at this date, could not supply such manpower.

To check whether there really was a temple here, the only thing to do was to remove the sand from beneath the head identified by Burckhardt as belonging to Osiris (and which belonged, in fact, to the god of the dawn, Re-Horakhte), and to slide in through the doorway – if indeed there was a doorway. It was at this point that those consuls-cum-antiquarians – Bernardino Drovetti and Henry Salt – suddenly reappeared on the scene. Burckhardt's account had drawn them like a magnet and they were determined to find a way inside the

temple, convinced of the treasures it concealed.

Drovetti was the first to arrive, reaching Abu Simbel in March 1816. For the sum of 300 piastres, he eventually managed to persuade the village sheikh to have some men begin clearing away the sand while Drovetti himself went on to Wadi Halfa to see the Great Cataract. On his return, a few days later, nothing had been done. The villagers were superstitious and had refused to work, fearing the misfortunes that might befall them if they tried to enter the temple. The sheikh gave back the money and Drovetti left.

Salt, for his part, asked Belzoni, who was then in Luxor, to take charge of the operation. On his arrival at Abu Simbel in September 1816, Belzoni sized up the difficulties of the situation. To clear the entire façade would require at least a year, and a massive workforce. He had neither the time, the manpower nor the money for it. It was clear, therefore, that he should concentrate all his efforts on the potential doorway between the two central colossi. To reach this door, Belzoni calculated that he would have to remove 35 feet (more than 10 metres) of sand, while more sand continued to pour relentlessly down from the clifftop, forcing him, in his own words, 'to try and make a hole in water'. Nevertheless, he attempted to set up a stockade to hold back the flow of the sand, and to dampen the walls of the hole as he made his way down. After a week of proceeding in this fashion, he had not reached half the necessary depth and he had run out of money. He decided to return to Luxor.

It was a year later that Belzoni returned to Abu Simbel, this time in the company of two Royal Navy captains, Mangles and Irby and Henry Beechey. Using the same methods as in 1816, after almost three weeks of back-breaking effort they discovered the top of a doorway on 1 August. Creating a narrow passage between the lintel and the cleared sand, they slipped down into the interior. As they did so, a vast area opened up before their eyes. Belzoni has left an enthusiastic account of what he now saw. Despite his enthusiasm, however, Belzoni was to be bitterly disappointed: this magnificent temple contained none of the treasures he had been hoping for, only a few small monuments, stelae and statues which he could take away with him.

Their provisions had run out and Belzoni and his companions left Abu Simbel on 4 August 1817, three days after being the first to enter it. They left the opening they had made and asked the neighbouring villagers to keep it free.

Despite their instructions, however, the sand – assisted by the local people – was to conceal the temple entrance for a long time to come.

In 1828 Champollion had to open up a narrow passage to get to the sanctuary

In 1831, thanks to the efforts of the Englishman Robert Hay, the four colossi were entirely visible for the first time; but, in March 1850, when Maxime du Camp, who was travelling with his friend Gustave Flaubert, took the first photographs of the temple, the doorway was half blocked and the colossi were once more largely buried in sand. In 1869 it was Mariette's turn to clear the façade, but five years later, when Amelia Edwards visited Abu Simbel, the northern statues were once more concealed from view. The battle with the sand seemed doomed to failure. It was not until Gaston Maspero applied himself to the task in 1909 that the temple was cleared of its burden for good.

Jean Vercoutter

Stories of pillaging

All those treasures lying buried in the heart of the tombs were irresistible. Treasure hunting began well before the arrival of the Europeans and 'How To' guides to the perfect tomb robbery were already in circulation in Muslim Egypt. And, though the methods may have changed, some Egyptian peasants still succumb to the temptation, even today.

In this book you will find a description of the hiding places and the treasures of Egypt and of the land round about. We have copied this from the books of our ancestors and passed it on in their own words, convinced of their truthfulness, as proved by the preciseness of their instructions.

The Great Pyramid of Giza

From this pyramid, walk north-westward and you will come to a white mountain, beneath which there runs a path leading to a depression made in soft ground. Make a fumigation with tar, liquid styrax and black sheep's wool, and you will see a pathway surrounding four *feddans* of earth. Keep the smoke blowing from your fumigation and cross the pathway. Then dig down into the earth to a cubit's depth and you will find piles of refined gold. Take as much of it as you wish, but do not allow your fumigation to die down until you have finished.

The opening of the Great Pyramid at Giza

Make your way towards the sphinx and measure out twelve Malekite cubits (one Malekite cubit being the equivalent of one and a half cubits measured by a man's forearm) in a south-easterly direction from its face; there you will find a heap of stones. Dig right in the centre of the two *mastabas*, to the depth of a *qamah* and a *bastah*, and you will discover a trapdoor. Clear away all the sand from on top of this and, raising it up, proceed towards the door of the Great Pyramid. Step over the threshold, paying attention meanwhile to the closed wells to right and left, since you must respect these wells and walk straight ahead without touching them, or you will have cause to regret it. As you enter this place, you will find a large stone.

Move this stone aside and pass through into another place, where you will see, to right and left, many rooms and, before you, a large hall containing the body of one of the first kings of Egypt. This king is surrounded by other kings and by his son, all of them clothed in gowns embroidered with gold thread and decorated with precious stones. Close by them you will see piles of silver, rubies, fine pearls, and gold and silver statues and idols. In this mountain [of jewels] you must search for a recess richly inlaid in wood and enclosing a grotto. In this grotto you will see a large monolith which you will be able to move to one side, and thereby reveal a well containing a great deal of silver deposited there by the pagans. Take as much of it as you wish. God is most wise.

The Book of Buried Pearls
Written in Arabic before the 16th century

In February 1817 Belzoni left Bulak, then a suburb of Cairo, with the intention of excavating the Theban tombs cut into the mountainside at Gourna.

Explorations in the Gourna tombs

Of some of these tombs many persons could not withstand the suffocating air, which often causes fainting. A vast quantity of dust rises, so fine that it enters into the throat and nostrils, and chokes the nose and mouth to such a degree, that it requires great power of lungs to resist it and the strong effluvia of the mummies. This is not all; the entry or passage where the bodies are is roughly cut in the rocks, and the falling of the sand from the upper part or ceiling of the passage causes it to be nearly filled up. In some places there is not more than a vacancy of a foot left, which you must contrive to pass through in a creeping posture like a snail, on pointed and keen stones, that cut like glass. After getting through these passages, some of them two or three hundred yards long, you generally find a more commodious place, perhaps high enough to sit. But what a place of rest! surrounded by bodies, by heaps of mummies in all directions; which, previous to my being accustomed to the sight, impressed me with horror. The blackness of the wall, the faint light given by the candles or torches for want

Travellers loved to describe visits to underground tombs; but these were often a source of disappointment: either the tombs were empty or the objects they contained were, in the visitor's eyes, worthless.

of air, the different objects that surrounded me, seeming to converse with each other, and the Arabs with the candles or torches in their hands, naked and covered with dust, themselves resembling living mummies, absolutely formed a scene that cannot be described. In such a situation I found myself several times, and often returned exhausted and fainting, till at last I became inured to it, and indifferent to what I suffered, except from the dust, which never failed to choke my throat and nose; and though, fortunately, I am destitute of the sense of smelling, I could taste that the mummies were rather unpleasant to swallow. After the exertion of entering into such a place, through a passage of fifty, a hundred, three hundred, or perhaps six hundred yards, nearly overcome, I sought a resting-place, found one, and contrived to sit; but when my weight bore on the body of an Egyptian, it crushed it like a band-box. I naturally had recourse to my hands to sustain my weight, but they found no better support; so that I sunk altogether among the broken mummies, with a crash of bones, rags, and wooden cases, which raised such a dust as kept me motionless for a quarter of an hour, waiting till it subsided again. I could not remove from the place, however, without increasing it, and every step I took I crushed a mummy in some part or other. Once I was conducted from such a place to another resembling it, through a passage of about twenty feet in length, and no wider than that a body could be forced through. It was choked with mummies, and I could not pass without putting my face in contact with that of some decayed Egyptian; but as the passage inclined downwards, my own weight helped me on: however, I could not avoid being covered with bones, legs, arms, and heads rolling from above.

Thus I proceeded from one cave to another, all full of mummies piled up in various ways, some standing, some lying, and some on their heads. The purpose of my researches was to rob the Egyptians of their papyri; of which I found a few hidden in their breasts, under their arms, in the space above the knees, or on the legs, and covered by the numerous folds of cloth, that envelop the mummy.

Belzoni, *Egypt and Nubia,* 1820

In 1945 the Egyptian architect Hassan Fathy was given the job of building an important village, that of New Gourna, near Luxor. The village was to rehouse around seven thousand people who had been living on the site of the ancient tombs of Thebes.

There are seven thousand peasants living in Gourna, all massed together in five clusters of houses built on and around the tombs – seven thousand people living, literally, on the past. It was these richly furnished tombs of their ancestors which attracted them – or their fathers before them – to Gourna some fifty-odd years ago. The land around the site could not feed seven thousand people, most of it belonging to a handful of wealthy individuals, and their economy depended almost entirely on robbing the tombs.

Although the Gournis had developed an unrivalled expertise in the location of tombs and were adept in the art of robbing them, they had failed to manage their industry efficiently. They had extracted their treasures before antiquities began to fetch a high price. Hakim Abu Seif, an inspector in the Antiquities Service, told me that in 1913 a peasant had offered him a basket full of scarabs for twenty piastres, and that he had refused it. Today a single scarab fetches five pounds.

Deir el-Bahari prior to excavations.

One must not suppose that the looting was limited to scarabs alone, or that all the peasants were quite so naive. When an 18th-dynasty tomb, that of Amenophis II, was discovered [in 1893], a sacred boat was stolen by one of the guards [in 1901], who later set himself up on forty acres of land thanks to the proceeds of his theft.

We should not take the activities of these robbers too lightly, however. For, despite all their skill and dexterity, and their very real poverty, they did immeasurable damage. They dug, and sold the products of their digging, and – to the huge detriment of archaeology – no one knew the actual origin of their finds. Worse still, if by chance one of these robbers found an item in gold, they would melt it down. Jewels, plaques, statuettes – priceless masterpieces – all went straight into the kilns and were transformed into crude bullion that was then sold at the market price. Those pieces that have survived – among them, the treasures of Tutankhamun's tomb and the marvellously worked dishes

recently discovered at Tanis – give us some idea of the scale of the destruction.

The peasants naturally fell prey to middlemen from the towns, who alone had the means of communicating with unscrupulous foreign buyers, and were in a position to exploit the Gournis' delicate situation by buying their priceless finds well below their actual value. The peasants took all the risks, developing their skill and doing the hard work, while the middlemen encouraged the vandalism, in perfect safety, enriching themselves on the hard-earned fruits of the Gournis' labour.

In the end, the decreasing yield on their stolen goods forced the villagers to take greater and greater risks and to carry out increasingly daring excavations (refining their skills in the process), until at last the situation erupted with an unprecedented scandal. A whole section of sculpted rock – a famous, classified ancient monument – was cut away from the mountainside and stolen. It was as if someone had stolen a window from Chartres Cathedral or a couple of columns from the Parthenon.

The theft caused so many repercussions that the Antiquities Service was forced to take concrete steps with regard to Gourna. According to an existing royal decree, the Gournis had no rights to the land on which their houses were built, and the entire sector of the necropolis was annexed and classified as an area of public utility. This decree gave the Gournis the right to continue to use their existing homes but prohibited any extension or additional construction. A second ministerial decree had to be drawn up depriving them of the use of their homes altogether, thereby freeing the area of its undesirable squatters.

Hassan Fathy
Building with the People, Editions Sindbad

Egyptology today

Less than a hundred years have passed since the great individual expeditions; now Egyptology's emphasis has shifted to scientific study and team work. Archaeologists spend part of their life in the field, of course, but the rest is confined to the study and the laboratory. Rarely working in isolation, they set their own researches alongside those of specialists, or technicians, engaged in other fields. And once in a lifetime, perhaps, an archaeologist may experience the intense emotions that derive from the discovery of a new site.

The antechamber in Maya's tomb.

The time is long past when enlightened – and wealthy – patrons and amateurs like Theodore Davis and the Earl of Carnarvon were free to begin excavating a site almost at will. Only government bodies are in a position to obtain concessions for excavations and to fund the work on an important site. In general it is the permanent Egyptological institutes, set up either in Egypt or abroad, which organize such digs and scientific research. Today twenty-six countries have at least one research centre – and in some cases several – specializing in Egyptology attached to either a university or a museum, and in some cases several. Egypt itself takes an active part in this work. The inspectors of the Egyptian Antiquities Organization, the successor of Mariette and Maspero's Antiquities Service, provide help to foreign missions in the field. The general inspectors for Upper, Middle and Lower Egypt have a responsibility for the sites and monuments in their own area and, where necessary, organize any rescue work to be undertaken. The big universities, notably Cairo, Assiut and Alexandria, also have their own sites. Finally, Egypt has two important Egyptological documentation centres, one in Cairo and the other, a Franco-Egyptian institute, at Karnak.

Interest in Egyptology has thus developed on a large scale since the 19th century, when Egyptologists all knew one another personally and exchanged letters and information. A few years ago an International Association of Egyptologists was set up and at a recent count it had some nine hundred members! Overall thousands of books and articles have been published on Egyptology. As a result it is becoming more and more difficult to have a thorough knowledge of the subject and

Egyptology, like many other sciences, is tending to become compartmentalized, dividing into philology, epigraphy, history and history of religion on the one hand and archaeology and history of art on the other.

Moreover, Egyptologists, working alongside prehistorians, have gradually become familiarized with the rigorous methods of new archaeology. Nowadays they are no longer content merely to study written documents and artefacts, as was too often the case before. They know that a close examination and analysis of the layers of the soil which they are excavating can teach them as much as, if not more than, the longest inscription on a stele or a monument wall. In the last fifteen years or so, thanks to modern scientific methods and laboratory studies, Egyptology has thus seen its field of research widely extended.

We must not assume, however, that because of these new approaches, discoveries like those of the Serapeum, Tutankhamun's tomb or the royal tombs at Tanis are now an impossibility. Man has lived in the Nile valley and its oases, and crossed the neighbouring deserts, for so many thousands of years that he has left traces of his presence everywhere, and many of them still remain undiscovered. Nor should we forget that the various capitals which have dominated Egypt at different times in its history have never been fully explored.... And, finally, we are still ignorant of the whereabouts of many of the pharaohs' tombs; even that of Alexander the Great has yet to be discovered!

Jean Vercoutter

The rediscovery of Maya's tomb

The tomb of Tutankhamun's treasurer, Maya, was known to 19th-century archaeologists including the German Karl Richard Lepsius, who drew some of the reliefs in 1843. Although he did not penetrate into the underground burial chambers, Lepsius nevertheless marked the rough location of the tomb on his published map of the area. In subsequent years the tomb disappeared beneath drifts of sand and the site was lost.

On 8 February 1986 Geoffrey T. Martin of University College London and Jacobus Van Dijk of the Leyden Museum were excavating on behalf of the Egypt Exploration Society in the necropolis at Saqqara. At the bottom of a shaft, through an ancient robbers' tunnel, they discovered a funerary antechamber decorated with inscriptions and reliefs: they had found the tomb of Maya and of his wife, Merit.

The two archaeologists – to whom we also owe the discovery, in 1975, of the nearby tomb of Horemhab – had Lepsius' map to thank for leading them to the famous treasurer's tomb, but that in no way detracts from the significance of their find. This time the tomb is to be throroughly cleared, excavated, and studied in meticulous detail, and will undoubtedly shed light on the little-known period of Egyptian history at the close of the 18th dynasty. Maya was not only a royal scribe and treasurer to Tutankhamun, he was also accorded the honour of providing some funeral gifts for the pharaoh and had the responsibility of burying him in the Valley of the Kings. Moreover, he continued to hold office during the reign of Ay (1343 BC) and at the beginning of the reign of Horemheb (1340-1314 BC), the young pharaoh's successors.

Science and the Future, April 1986

A new lease of life for Ramesses II

In 1976 a team of 102 scientists bent their efforts to saving the ailing mummy of this famous pharaoh and restored him to his place among the immortals. The body of Ramesses II now lies in the Cairo Museum, and his gaze is fastened once more on eternity.

After thirty centuries of a journey in both time and space, he has come home again: to the museum at Cairo. Making a fitting return to his roots. His face – sharply drawn in profile, softened by a few brittle strands of wavy blond hair, once dyed with henna – has an all-knowing look. His hands, bound in lengths of ancient linen with no pin, no stitch to hold them together, are long and slender. Like his hair, his amber nails are coloured still with henna, symbol of life. Ramesses was a Mediterranean, and, in death, he has retained all the anthropological characteristics of his race. There is a golden transparency to his skin, and he appears to be sleeping, deeply and peacefully. Looking at him it is hard to imagine, in fact, that this frail, willowy body breathed its last breath so very long ago. His features have such a living quality, his flesh seems so intact, that one is torn between amazement and something akin to fear.

In 1976 the picture was quite different.... There was something wrong with the mummy of Ramesses II, the most famous pharaoh known to Egypt. Century after century it had resisted the ravages of time, but now it manifested all the disturbing signs of some creeping, insidious illness. What was the source of this invisible disease that showed so little respect for persons? How could it be eradicated for good and the divine Ramesses be restored to his sovereign immortality?

For seven months, on the initiative of Christiane Desroches-Noblecourt, today Honorary Inspector of French Museums, and thanks to the support of the top authorities in Egypt and France, a team of 102 scientists focused their attention on Ramesses' plight. The team was directed by Dean Lionel Balout, administrator of the Musée de l'Homme

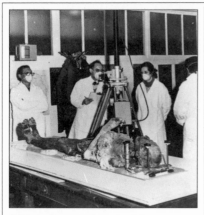

Technicians seen here, in a laboratory at the Musée de l'Homme, taking photogrammetric measurements of Ramesses II's body.

in Paris, and his collaborator, Professor Colette Roubert, assistant director of the museum.

A third life for Ramesses II

It was September 1976. The mummy of Ramesses II was in Paris. The scientists who had taken charge of him were silent, overcome with emotion. Behind their surgeons' masks, they held their breath; for this patient was so famous, so prestigious.... A wave of anxiety swept over them, born of the magnitude of the task that lay ahead. Lying stretched out in a simple oak coffin, stripped of all the trappings of his glory, Ramesses was now just a sick old man.

According to Egyptologists, this mighty king was probably born in *c.* 1279 BC, in the Theban palace of Seti I, his father and predecessor. He died nearly seventy years later, in *c.* 1212, and his body was embalmed in accordance with the sacred rites to which only the pharaohs were entitled. His mummy,

wrapped in cloth and decorated with jewels, was laid to rest in the Valley of the Kings. Two centuries later, robbers broke into his tomb and stole all the treasures adorning the king's body, including the gold plaque which the embalmers had placed over the embalming incision in his abdominal cavity. Pinedjem, the High Priest of Amun and ruler of Thebes during the 21st dynasty, had the mummy restored and necklaces of lotus flowers and waterlilies placed round its neck.... Ramesses II thus renewed his ties with eternity for the second time.

In 1000 BC the body of Ramesses was concealed, along with a number of other royal mummies, in the cliffs at Deir el-Bahari. And there it remained until 1881, when it was discovered by a local peasant and identified by the French Egyptologist Gaston Maspero. The pharaoh had lost all the insignia of royalty, but he still had a small roll of papyrus attached to his breast.

In 1912 x-rays showed the English Egyptologist Sir Grafton Eliott Smith that the body of Ramesses II was deteriorating.... Sixty-five years later, the damage had spread, and the mummy needed attention more urgently than ever.

Ramesses II, victim of a fungus

From the moment of his arrival in Paris, scientists worked assiduously to save Ramesses. The first task was to determine the exact cause of his illness. Among the remains of the linen wrappings, some samples of minute fragments from the mummy's chest and some fallen hairs were collected and immediately analysed in the specialized laboratories of the Musée d'Histoire Naturelle, the Identité Judiciaire, the Institut Textile de France, L'Oreal, the CNRS and the

An enlargement of the fungus culture taken from the mummy. Finally a treatment was found and the mummy (opposite) was cured of the mysterious illness.

Commissariat à l'Energie Atomique. Was it bacteria? Fungus? Insects? The experts all brought their most sophisticated microscopes to bear on the problem.... It was Dr Jean Mouchacca, a cryptogam specialist at the Musée d'Histoire Naturelle, who succeeded in identifying the destructive organism: a fungus with the preposterous name of *Daedalea biennis Fries.* The first stage was over....

By probing further and further into his secrets, the team had begun to feel a certain closeness to the old pharaoh, and they were all delighted with the discovery. In tandem with this research other tests had been carried out, completing those already undertaken at Cairo. These had brought the scientists new insights into the life of Ramesses II and enabled them to identify the cause of his death. Methods used included radiology and x-ray, endoscopy, chromodensitography, bacteriology, palynology, palaeobotany, tests on samples and on the mummy itself and gamma radiation using cobalt-60.

The in-depth study of Ramesses' skeleton, the walls of his femoral arteries, his teeth, and his whole mummified body, proved highly revealing. It appears that Ramesses suffered from a slight limp and a stiffening of the spinal column, and that his head was inclined too far forward in relation to his spine. When he was buried, the embalmers straightened his head, causing visible fracturing to the front and back of his neck. The pharaoh had numerous abscesses in his teeth and all the evidence suggests that he died as a result of a general infection.

Uncovering the cause of Ramesses' illness was one thing; saving him was quite another. Lionel Balout and Colette Roubet knew this only too well. It was time to act and to arrest the problem using all the means that modern technology placed at their disposal. Chemotherapy, and any kind of process using heat or cold, were quickly dismissed as possibilities. The reason for this was that no one knew how the resins and gums employed during the embalming process would react to such treatments: there were too many imponderables. Only one solution remained: to subject Ramesses II to radiation treatment. It was a difficult decision for which to take sole responsibility. If the pharaoh were even the slightest bit damaged, diplomatic relations with the Egyptians would no doubt suffer.

From the start of the operation the mummy was handled with the utmost care and remained under the watchful eye of Dr Sawki Nakhla, Egypt's official representative. The base of the oak coffin, the vehicle in which the king had been travelling, was cut away so that a sheet of altuglas could be slid under the body and this then transferred to an operating table. The head and torso were propped up with small cushions to avoid putting any strain on the skeleton, and the body was only exposed while the scientists were working on it, and then

never for more than three hours at a stretch....

The key word, therefore, was caution. The scientists had no option but to take action, however. Jean Mouchacca's diagnosis was quite explicit: if they failed to eradicate the fungus, by the end of the century Ramesses II's mummy would be entirely eaten up by it. Dean Balout alone was in a position to decide on the form of treatment that should be applied. His verdict: radiation.

It was at the Centre d'Etudes Nucleaires in Grenoble and in the laboratories headed by Robert Cornuet that a lengthy series of samples taken from Ramesses (fungus, hair, cloth fragments) and from another mummy (various human tissues) were tested and treated with gamma radiation using cobalt-60. The results were highly encouraging. The tests had no effect on either human tissue or hair. Here, then, was a chance.... for to return Ramesses to the Egyptians minus his few blond locks would have been unthinkable. The action of the rays was sufficiently powerful, on the other hand, to succeed in destroying the fungus. This first experiment was followed by another whereby a 'martyr mummy' was subjected to the same 'regime'. This second operation was carried out by CEA technicians at the Centre Nucleaire at Saclay, near Paris. Once again the process was a hundred per cent successful. Ramesses, it seemed, was on the verge of a cure.

Ramesses II was first restored, with infinite care, by the specialists at the Musée de l'Homme, then draped in a piece of antique linen cloth courtesy of the Louvre and placed in his cedarwood coffin. He had been reborn a second time and recovered all his former radiance. The doctors who tended him merely played the same part that the priests had played before them. Respecting ancient religious tradition, they had given Ramesses' spirit the dwelling it desired: a perfect body. And from within this frail frame the king gazes down now on the river of life. He has just signed a new contract with eternity.

Sygma

In search of Cheops

Have we still not found the real Great Pyramid? According to two French architects, the answer is no. Excavations, begun in 1986, searched for evidence to support their theory.

Was the mass of Cheops' pyramid merely a blind to deceive intruders? A skilfully executed stage set, designed by an ingenious architect, to shield the secrets of the royal tomb? Do another entrance, other passageways, other cavities and perhaps even another King's Chamber, exist within the bulk of the Great Pyramid?

It is an intriguing theory, to which two architects, Gilles Dormion and Jean-Patrice Goidin (both working in Lille), seriously subscribe. And it has won over the Quai d'Orsay [the French Foreign Ministry] and the Egyptian authorities. With the help of the EDF and of the Compagnie de Prospection Géophysique Française, the two architects began investigations in the Great Pyramid on 28 August 1986.

It all came about by chance. The two men were old friends and both were scuba-diving fanatics. An expedition to the Red Sea sparked off an interest in Egypt and, on their return home, a mutual friend gave them a copy of Edgar P. Jacobs' comic strip *The Mystery of the Great Pyramid.*

Gilles Dormion was fascinated by some of the minute details of the illustrations. He was particularly curious about the strange slots featured on both walls of the Great Gallery. What, he wondered, could be the purpose of these grooves running the length of both walls?

He was equally surprised to see markings halfway up, surrounded by numerous stone chippings. The two architects sought explanations for these phenomena in specialist books on the subject, but found no satisfactory answers.

They continued to look for answers, initially out of idle curiosity, and soon became thoroughly engrossed in the search. By sifting photographs and

T he first stage: the team inspecting the entrance to the Great Pyramid.

Jean-Pierre Baron drilling in the corridor to the Queen's Chamber.

documents, they made up a file of measurements and surveys, comparing their finds with the data given for other pyramids. And, as they did so, further anomalies came to light.

The two architects were aware that such oddities could not be constructional errors. The Egyptians knew the rules of architecture too well to tolerate unnecessary details or imperfections. According to Dormion and Goidin, all these points had been planned in advance, with a purpose.

Prompted by this realization, Dormion and Goidin spent several months trying to rediscover the logic behind the pyramid's construction.

They were entirely on their own, and groping in the dark: attempts to convince Egyptologists of their theory met with blank rejection.

They would have gone on struggling for months had not, in December 1985, an American team begun investigations in the pyramid of Cheops in an effort to locate a solar barque. Afraid of having their discoveries stolen from under their noses, they decided to reveal all to M. Philippe Guillemin, assistant director of social and human affairs at the Quai d'Orsay.

Guillemin was fascinated by their theory, but nevertheless sought advice. He passed their material on to M. Yves Boiret, chief architect of the Bâtiments de France, and to M. Bernard Maury, a specialist in Islamic architecture. The former showed a keen interest in the matter and Maury even went so far as to request that he be allowed to join the team conducting the initial investigations. The Egyptian authorities were equally enthusiastic.

The two architects had opened up a whole new approach to Egyptology and the logic on which their theories were based appeared to explain the Great Pyramid's entire system of construction.

The anomalies were apparent from the moment one entered the pyramid. Access to the burial chamber was via a low opening, similar to those found in other pyramids. But why build four enormous lintels across the top of the chamber, and protect these in turn with two gigantic blocks, to form a pointed roof?

Dormion and Goidin speculated, in fact, that this huge structure might possibly mask another entrance, one that had been closed off since the pharaoh's death.

In part of the Ascending Corridor,

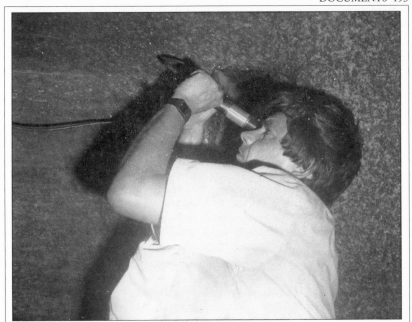

An endoscope is inserted into a bore hole in the wall of the King's Chamber.

they also observed a series of strange girdle stones running the length of the walls. They had seen nothing like them elsewhere in the pyramid. According to archaeologists, the purpose of this system was to resist lateral pressure exerted on the walls. The two architects had a different theory, but no desire to share it just yet.

Continuing on up, one reaches the Great Gallery with its wall slots and corbelled roof – it was the former element which first attracted the attention of the two architects. Gilles Dormion did a few quick sketches to explain their function to me. 'The slots could have supported scaffolding erected up to the ceiling. Beyond that there would have been a series of cavities.

Before the tomb was closed up for the last time, the Great Gallery would have been the setting for a major architectural juggling act.'

The portcullis corridor, situated at the top of the Great Gallery, also housed some surprises. Its purpose was to prevent access to the King's Chamber by means of three granite portcullises. However, to reach the sarcophagus, all one had to do was to climb on to the stone placed in front of the portcullises and clamber over the top of them, then break off a corner of the granite block theoretically barring the entrance to the King's Chamber. This, at any rate, was the method employed, in 820, by the Caliph al Ma'mun, when he came to steal the contents of the King's Chamber.

A strange way of sealing a pharaoh's tomb, to be sure!

Pharaohs of the New Kingdom opted, like Tutankhamun, for concealment in the Valley of the Kings as the best means of protecting their tombs against potential thieves. Cheops, on the other hand [a thousand years earlier], had elected to build a pyramid exposed to the eyes of the world. And that made a reliable system of protection all the more important. Why then did the architect design such a patently insecure structure? And why too did he provide the portcullis corridor with a double sliding portcullis?

The King's Chamber is built of enormous blocks of granite and, by its impressive size, apparently conforms to the pattern of a royal tomb. What is more surprising, however, is the series of relieving chambers (four in all) formed by gigantic lintels over the top of the King's Chamber. According to Egyptologists, the purpose of this 2500-ton stone pile is to counterbalance lateral pressure. Hence, the name 'relieving chamber'. However, these rooms are constructed in such a way that they relieve no structural tension whatsoever.

The vaulted ceiling above them, however, does indeed fulfil this function, dispersing pressure in a lateral direction. 'The stone stacking', notes M. Dormion, 'could be a means of raising the height of the ceiling. A space at either side is thereby freed of all weight. And it is here that the King's Chamber could be concealed.'

The architects proceeded to investigate other parts of the pyramid. It struck them that the stonework in the Queen's Corridor had been assembled in a peculiar way, and they thought it could conceal a number of side chambers.

The first excavations began last May.

On awkward terrain like this, only a limited range of equipment could be used. EDF, in association with the Compagnie de Prospection Géophysique Française, opted for gravimetry, a technique for measuring relative densities. The first results obtained were encouraging. In the Queen's Corridor, the equipment registered gravimetric irregularities – just where the architects had anticipated they might occur. Such 'vacuums' might possibly correspond to cavities: Dormion and Goidin's hypothetical side chambers.

The surveys carried out in the relieving chambers were less conclusive, as Dormion acknowledged: 'We did register some anomalies, but they are difficult to interpret. Besides which, there are a few measurements missing for the King's Chamber and one or two of the relieving chambers.'

In all events the directors of the Egyptian Antiquities Organization in Cairo regarded these first tests as sufficiently conclusive to warrant a concession to excavate. The team's first job will be to verify the existence of the 'storerooms' or side chambers using a sophisticated technique known as microboring. This involves making tiny bore holes in the walls and taking photographs of the area behind them by inserting an endoscope with a minute camera attached.

Assuming that these first tests are successful, the team could go on and apply the same technique in other parts of the pyramid. And, whether evidence is found to support it or not, the architects' theory will have done much towards furthering the development of Egyptological research.

The techniques used here will enable archaeologists to discover, for the first time, the systems upon which the

Egyptians' building methods were based. Without disturbing a thing.

Martine Orange
Topical Values, 1 September 1986

February 1987: A Japanese team detect further cavities in the Great Pyramid.

A Japanese team, led by Sakuji Yoshimura, professor at Tokyo's Wascola University, has just discovered the existence of further cavities in the corridor leading to the Queen's Chamber and around the Great Pyramid....

A method of detection using microgravimetry, registering the relative densities in the walls of the Great Pyramid, had been used in different sections of the pyramid. Major abnormalities in the densitometric graphs had then led the French team to make three little holes in the west face of the Queen's Corridor. A strange crystalline sand had accumulated there....

The Japanese technique is similar to that of the scanner: electromagnetic waves were transmitted through the west wall of the Queen's Corridor, then the echo, picked up by a rather bulky aerial, was analysed using a microcomputer. The presence of a vacuum alongside the chamber was seen as blue patches on the grid; but Professor Yoshimura is still puzzled by a number of little red dots that occurred in the middle of the blue patches. 'Whereas microgravimetry can be said to weigh the vacuum,' Gilles Dormion, one of the two architects responsible for the original research in this area, stresses, 'microwaves actually give you an impression of it. In the last few weeks, we have also been studying the possibility of a microwave approach.'

The microwave method is more refined than microgravimetry but has a narrower 'sweep', so that the two methods would seem to be

Sakuji Yoshimura (right).

complementary. This, at least, is what the EDF are banking on. They intend to continue taking soundings of the relative densities within Cheops' pyramid, and around it and the Sphinx – where the Japanese have also found 'geometric' cavities filled with sand and possibly interconnecting, as in the case of other Egyptian sites. Used seven years ago for the Paris Metro and the RER, the microwave technique continues to pose problems. 'The interpretation is the difficult thing', Claude Dutems, of the Bureau d'Etude de l'Entretien à la RATP, emphasizes: 'It is easy to confuse a change in material with an empty space.' The difficulty is one the Japanese have not yet resolved.

This new cavity has been estimated as being 2 m deep by 4 m high, but, to know more, we will have to wait for 15 April, by which time Sakuji Yoshimura's team will have carried out a more sophisticated analysis....

Vincent Tardieu, *Liberation*, 4 February 1987

[In 1989 the Egyptian Antiquities Organization forbade further microboring.]

Pre-dynastic period
6000-3100 BC

No building work, but numerous stone tools and decorated pottery.

Archaic or 'Thinite' period
c. 3100-2890 BC

1st dynasty: c. 3200-2850. Eight pharaohs, from Menes (Narmer) to Qaa.	Large brick tombs at Hierakonpolis, Abydos and Saqqara. Development of writing.
2nd dynasty: c. 2890-2686. Six pharaohs, from Hetepsekhemui to Khasekhemui.	

Old Kingdom or Memphite empire
c. 2686

3rd dynasty: c. 2686-2613. Five pharaohs, from Neterikhet-Djoser to Huni.	Beginning of stone architecture. Djoser's Step Pyramid built at Saqqara.
4th dynasty: c. 2613-2494. Six or seven pharaohs, from Snefru to Shepeskaf, including Cheops, Chephren and Mykerinus.	Large pyramids and mortuary complex with: Valley temple, causeway leading to the mortuary temple attached to the east face of the pyramid.
5th dynasty: c. 2494-2345. Nine pharaohs, from Userkaf to Unas. The best known are Sahure and Djedkare-Isesi.	Royal solar temples with obelisk and monumental altar. Decorated *mastabas* for important officials.
6th dynasty: c. 2345-2181. Seven pharaohs, from Teti I to Queen Nitocris. Pepi I and the centenarian Pepi II belonged to this dynasty.	Development of inscriptions inside the pyramids (pyramid texts). Governors' tombs in the nomes (provincial administrative areas).

First intermediate period
c. 2181-2060

A time of anarchy, followed by a period during which Egypt was governed by two separate dynasties, one operating in the north, the other in the south.

7th dynasty: Almost certainly fictitious. According to Manetho, 70 kings reigned during this dynasty, for a total of 70 days.	No known monuments.
8th dynasty: c. 2181-2130. Ruled from Memphis. According to the sources, it numbered between 8 and 27 rulers (of uncertain and, in some cases, unknown name).	Few monuments other than Ibi's pyramid at Saqqara.
9th-10th dynasties: c. 2130-2040. **North.** Ruled from Herakleopolis, near the Fayuum. More than six pharaohs, including three Khetis.	
11th dynasty: c. 2130-1991. **South.** Ruled from Thebes. Three Antefs.	Rock-cut tombs in the western cliffs of Thebes.

Middle Kingdom or First Theban empire
c. 1991-1786

End of the 11th dynasty: c. 2060-2000. Three Mentuhoteps, the first of whom reunified Egypt in c. 2040.	Mortuary temple of Mentuhotep at Deir el-Bahari.
12th dynasty: c. 1991-1786. Seven pharaohs by the name of Amenemhat or Senusret. The dynasty ended with Queen Sobekneferure.	Hawara labyrinth. Chapel of Senusret I at Karnak. Large fortresses between the First and Second Cataract in Nubia. Royal statuary.

Second intermediate period *c.* 1786-1674		New Kingdom or Second Theban empire *c.* 1567-1085	
A little-documented period of political instability. An Asian people, the Hyksos, invaded Egypt and seized power.		**18th dynasty:** *c.* 1567-1320. Fourteen rulers, from Ahmosis to Horemheb, including four Tuthmoseses and four Amenhoteps. Queen Hatshepsut, Akhenaton (Amenhotep IV) and Tutankhamun all belonged to this dynasty.	Work begun on the great temple of Amun and Karnak. Temples at Luxor and Deir el-Bahari. Colossi of Memnon. Tombs in the Valley of the Kings, in particular Tutankhamun's. Tombs, stelae and statues at Tell el-Amarna (Nefertiti).
13th and 14th dynasties: *c.* 1786-1674. We know the names of some forty pharaohs, including several Sobekheteps. Some of them must have reigned simultaneously in North, South and Middle Egypt. From *c.* 1730, these kings served as vassals to the Hyksos pharaohs.	Numerous stelae and statues; otherwise no monuments known.		
15th and 16th Hyksos dynasties: *c.* 1674-1567. The 16th 'Little Hyksos' dynasty was confined to the eastern delta. There were five 'Great Hyksos' pharaohs, including one Khyan and two Apopis.	Statues and numerous scarabs, but no large monuments.	**19th dynasty:** *c.* 1320-1200. Nine pharaohs, the Ramessides, including Ramesses I and II and Seti I and II.	Temple at Karnak. Luxor obelisks and colossi. Ramesseum at Thebes. Large tombs in the Valley of the Kings and Valley of the Queens. Abu Simbel temples in Nubia and temple at Abydos.
		20th dynasty: *c.* 1200-1085. Ten pharaohs: Sethnakht and Ramesses III-XI.	Medinet Habu. Shrines and temples at Karnak and Luxor.
17th dynasty: *c.* 1674-1567. Fourteen rulers, vassals of the Hyksos, governed Thebes and the Theban region. The last three, Tao I, Tao II and Kamosis initiated the conflict with the northern Hyksos.	Theban tombs, including those of Sequenenre Tao II and of his wife, richly furnished with burial goods.		

Step pyramid at Saqqara (3rd dynasty).

Third intermediate period *c.* 1085-715	
Era of political confusion: the 'Tanite' pharaohs ruled northern Egypt from Tanis, while the south answered to the high priests of Amun.	
21st dynasty: *c.* 1085-945. Smendes, Psousennes I and II ruled from Tanis; Herihor and Pinedjem from Thebes.	Limited artistic activity.
22nd and 23rd (Libyan) dynasties: *c.* 945-715. Twelve pharaohs: Sheshonq I-V, Osorkon I-IV, Takelot I-III.	Royal tombs at Tanis. Monumental doorway in honour of Amun.
24th dynasty: *c.* 727-715. Founded at Sais by Tefnakht, who was succeeded by Bocchoris.	

Ethiopian and Saite renaissance *c.* 747-525	
25th (Ethiopian) dynasty: *c.* 747-656. Piankhi (Peye), Shabaka and Takarka.	Napata monuments at Gebel Barkal.
26th (Saite) dynasty: *c.* 664-525. Psammetichus I-III, Necho, Apries and Amasis.	Archaizing style in imitation of Old and Middle Kingdom models. Memphis Serapeum.
27th (Persian) dynasty: *c.* 525-404. Cambyses, Darius, Xerxes and Artaxerxes.	Decorative additions to Memphis Serapeum.

Last Egyptian dynasties *c.* 404-343	
28th dynasty: *c.* 404-399. One pharaoh: Amyrtaeus. **29th (Mendesian) dynasty:** *c.* 399-380. Five rulers, including two Nepherites, Psammutis and Achoris. **30th dynasty:** 380-343. Founded by Nectanebo I at Sebennytos. Three pharaohs: Nectanebo I and II and Teos.	

Second era of Persian rule 343-332	
Three pharaohs: Artaxerxes III, Arses and Darius III.	

Ptolemaic Egypt 305-330	
Egypt governed by Greek-speaking pharaohs, the Ptolemys (I-XV), and by their wives, several Berenices, Cleopatras and Arsinoes.	Construction or reconstruction of numerous temples at Dendera, Edfu, Kom Ombo and Philae.

Roman and Byzantine Egypt 30 BC-AD 639	
Octavian (later Augustus) conquered Egypt in 30 BC, although it had in fact been a Roman protectorate since 59 BC. In 641 came the Arab conquest.	Until AD 395 temples maintained and built in the Egyptian style by the Roman emperors. Temple of Isis on Philae closed in 550.

FURTHER READING

C. Aldred, *Akhenaten: King of Egypt*, 1988

—, *Egypt to the End of the Old Kingdom*, 1965

—, *Egyptian Art: In the Days of the Pharaohs 3100-320 BC*, 1980

—, *The Egyptians*, 1987

P. Amiet, *Art in the Ancient World*, 1981

C. Andrews, *Ancient Egyptian Jewellery*, 1990

G. Belzoni, *Narrative of the Operations and Recent Discoveries within the Pyramids, Temples, Tombs and Excavations, in Egypt and Nubia*, 1820

J. L. Burckhardt, *Travels in Nubia*, 1819

J. F. Champollion, *Lettre à M. Dacier*, 1822

—, *Lettres écrites de l'Egypte*, 1833

—, *Monuments de l'Egypte et de la Nubie*, 1845

M. Champollion-Figeac, *L'Obélisque de Louqsor transporté à Paris*, 1833

R. Clark, *Myth and Symbol in Ancient Egypt*, 1978

P. A. Clayton, *The Rediscovery of Ancient Egypt: Artists and Travellers in the 19th Century*, 1982

E. Combes, *Voyage en Egypte, en Nubie*, 1846

J. S. Curl, *The Egyptian Revival*, 1982

W. R. Dawson and E. P. Uphill, *Who Was Who in Egyptology*, 2nd ed., 1972

E. de Montule, *Travels in Egypt in 1818 and 1819*, 1823

Description de l'Egypte, 9 vols, 1809-1822

D. V. Denon, *Travels in Upper and Lower Egypt*, 1803

M. S. Drower, *Flinders Petrie: A Life in Archaeology*, 1985

A. B. Edwards, *A Thousand Miles up the Nile*, 1877

C. El Mahdy, *Mummies, Myth and Magic: In Ancient Egypt*, 1989

L. N. P. A. Forbin, *Travels in Egypt 1817-1818*, 1819

I. A. Ghali, *Vivant Denon ou la conquête du bonheur*, 1986

L. Greener, *The Discovery of Egypt*, 1966

W. Hamilton, *Aegyptiaca*, 1809

W. C. Hayes, *The Scepter of Egypt*, 2 vols, 1959

J. C. Herold, *Napoleon in Egypt*, 1963

C. Hobson, *Exploring the World of the Pharaohs: A Complete Guide to Ancient Egypt*, 1987

J.-M. Humbert, *L'Egyptomanie dans l'art occidental*, 1989

IFAO, *Un siècle de fouilles françaises en Egypte 1880-1980*, 1981

J. Irby and C. Mangles, *Travels in Egypt and Nubia*, 1823

T. G. H. James (ed.), *Excavating in Egypt: The Egypt Exploration Society 1882-1982*, 1982

J. Lacoutre, *Champollion: une vie de lumières*, 1988

N. L'Hôte, *L'Obélisque de Louqsor*, 1836

—, *Lettres de l'Egypte*, 1840

E. Le Roy Ladurie, (ed.), *Mémoires d'Egypte: hommage de l'Europe à Champollion*, 1990

K. R. Lepsius, *Denkmäler aus Aegypten und Aethiopien*, 6 pt. in 12 vols, 1849-59

—, *Discoveries in Egypt, Ethiopia, and the Peninsula of Sinai, in the years 1842-1845*, 2nd ed., 1853

M. Lurker, *The Gods and Symbols of Ancient Egypt: An Illustrated Dictionary*, 1982

A. Mariette, *Le Serapeum de Memphis*, 1856

—, *Voyage de la Haute-Egypte*, 1878-90

G. Martin, *The Hidden Tombs of Memphis: New Discoveries from the Time of Tutankhamun and Ramesses the Great*, 1991

L. Mayer, *Views in Egypt*, 1804

S. Mayes, *The Great Belzoni*, 1959

K. Mendelssohn, *The Riddle of the Pyramids*, 1986

A. C. T. E. Prisse d'Avennes, *Histoire de l'art égyptien*, 1858-77

S. Quirke and C. Andrews, *The Rosetta Stone: Facsimile Drawing with an Introduction and Translations*, 1989

N. Reeves, *The Complete Tutankhamun*, 1990

L. Reybaud, *Histoire de l'expédition française en Egypte*, 1828

J. J. Rifaud, *Voyages 1805-27*, 1830

D. Roberts, *Egypt and Nubia* (lithographs), 3 vols, 1846-50

T. Säve-Söderbergh (ed.), *Temples and Tombs of Ancient Nubia*, 1987

V. Seton-Williams and P. Stocks, *Egypt* (Blue Guide), 2nd ed., 1988

H. Vyse and J.S. Perring, *Operations carried on at the Pyramids of Gizeh*, 3 vols, 1840-42

J. G. Wilkinson, *General View of Egypt*, 1835

—, *Manners and Customs of the Ancient Egyptians*, 3 vols, 1837

J. A. Wilson, *Signs and Wonders upon Pharaoh: A History of American Egyptology*, 1964

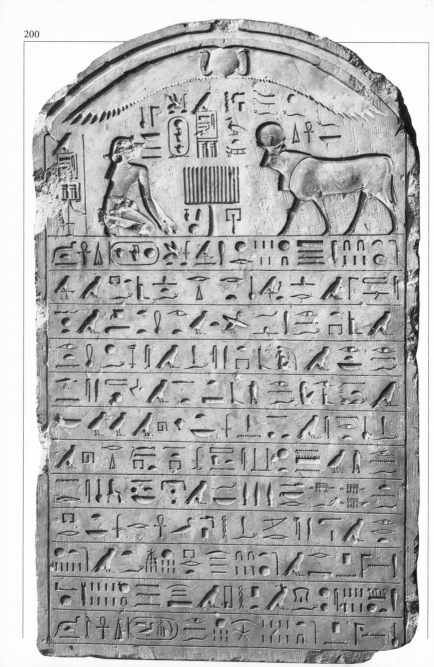

LIST OF ILLUSTRATIONS

INDEX

ACKNOWLEDGMENTS

We thank the following individuals and organizations for their help in producing this book: Mme. Abilès and M. Degardin, librarians at the Egyptology Department of the Collège de France; Peter Clayton; François Delebecque, photographer; (p. 159) John A. Wilson, *Signs and Wonders upon Pharaoh*, © 1964 The University of Chicago Press; M. Yoyotte from the Golenischeff Centre.

PHOTO CREDITS

Abbreviations: *a*, above; *b*, below; *c*, centre; *l*, left; *r*, right.

Artephot Bridgeman, Paris 2. Artephot/ Nimatallah, Paris 62*l*. Bib. Nat., Paris 15*a*, 17*r*, 20-21, 22*a*, 22*c*, 32*al*, 32*b*, 32*r*, 33*a*, 33*b*, 34-35, 54, 55*a*, 55*c*, 55*r*, 56-57, 58, 60*a*, 60*b*, 62*r*, 66-67, 69*l*, 69*r*, 96*a*, foldout 1, foldout 3, 130, 145*l*, 145*r*, 146, 164. Bridgeman Archives, London 83, 100. British Museum, London 19, 21*a*, 72, 91. Charmet, Paris 30*a*, 30*b*. All rights reserved 14-15, 18, 24*a*, 26*a*, 26*b*, 27, 36*a*, 36-37, 37*a*, 38*l*, 38*r*, 40-41, 42-43, 44-45, 46, 47, 50-51, 51*a*, 57*b*, 59, 61, 63*b*, 63*r*, 64-65, 66, 73*a*, 73*b*, 74-75, 76-77, 78-79, 80-81, 87, 88*a*, 88*b*, 89, 91, 92*a*, 92*b*, 93*b*, 94*a*, 94*c*, 95*a*, 95*b*, 96-97, 98, 99, 104, 106*b*, 107, 108*r*, 109*b*, 110, 111, 115*a*, 115*b*, 119*a*, 119*b*, 120*a*, 120*b*, 121*r*, 121*c*, 121*b*, 124*a*, 124*b*, 125*a*, 125*b*, 126*a*, 126*b*, 136, 138*a*, 138*bl*, 138*br*, 139, 140*a*, 140*b*, 141*a*, 141*cr*, 141*c*, 141*b*, 142*a*, 142*l*, 142*r*, 143*al*, 143*ar*, 144, 151*a*, 151*b*, 160, 161, 162*l*, 162*r*, 163*a*, 163*b*, 165, 167, 169, 171*a*, 176, 177, 178, 181, 183, 186, 197, 198. Edimédia, Paris 52, 53. Fotomas Index, London front cover. Giraudon, Paris 17*l*, 24-25, 28, 29, 48, 49, 86, 90, 101. Gallimard, l'Univers des Formes, Paris 23, 112, 113, 116*a*, 116*b*, 117*r*, 137. Kutshera, Monlivaut 31, 108*l*. Magnum, Paris 13. National Maritime Museum, Greenwich, London 148-149. Office du Livre, Fribourg 84-85. P. Clayton, London 12, 68*a*, 68*b*, 70-71, 82, 159. P. Bomhof, Leyde 184. P. Chuzeville, Louvre, Paris 200. P. Odiot, Paris 143*b*. Rapho, Paris 117*l*, 119*c*. RMN, Paris 65*a*, 94*b*, 102. Roger-Viollet, Paris 103, 109*l*, 109*r*, 114, 127, 129, 131, 133, 134, 147, 150, 157. Roger-Viollet, Harlingue, Paris 156. Scala, Florence 16. Sygma/A.D.P.F., Paris 187, 188. Sygma, Paris 189. The Illustrated London News 148*a*, 149*a*. Unesco/Vorontzoff, Paris 170, 170-171, 171*c*. Unesco Nenadovic, Paris 172, 173, 175. Unesco Ratke Hochtief, Paris 174*a*. Unesco/D. Roger, Paris 174*b*. Vu Descamps, Paris 190, 191, 192, 193, 195.

Jean Vercoutter
could have been a painter but he preferred
to be an archaeologist. He won a scholarship to
the 'school of Cairo' (the French Institute of
oriental archaeology) in 1939 but, because of the
Second World War, it was not until 1945 that he
actually arrived there. He took part in the
excavations at Karnak and then worked on
different sites in the Sudan which up till then had
been unexplored. In 1955 the Egyptians prepared
to build the new dam at Aswan. The ancient
monuments had to be saved as quickly as
possible. As director of the Antiquities Service at
Khartoum, Jean Vercoutter estimated that three
hundred sites were in danger. Thanks to a
tremendous international effort, the majority
were saved. During the 1960s Jean Vercoutter
was director of the Papyrological Institute at
Lille. In 1976 he was appointed professor at the
University and director of the Institut de Caire.
On 11 May 1984 he was elected to the Académie
des Inscriptions et Belles-Lettres of the
Institut de France.

For Victor, Akira and Thomas

© Gallimard 1986

English translation © Thames and Hudson Ltd,
London, and Harry N. Abrams, Inc., New York,
1992

Reprinted 1992, 1994 (twice), 1995, 1997

Translated by Ruth Sharman

ISBN 0–500–30013–5

Printed and bound in Italy by
Editoriale Libraria, Trieste